D0705985

ROMERO
&
GRANDE

COMPANIONS ON *THE JOURNEY*

Ana María Pineda, R.S.M.

lectio

Lectio Publishing, LLC
Hobe Sound, Florida, USA

www.lectiopublishing.com

© 2016, all rights reserved. No part of this book may be reproduced or transmitted in any form or by any means, electronic or mechanical, including photocopying or recording, or by any information storage and retrieval system without prior written permission of the publisher.

All translations, unless otherwise noted, are those of the author.

The image leading Chapter 7 is © Matthew Wettlaufer, and is used with permission.

All other photographs are from the author's personal collection of Salvadoran mural art photographed during various visits to El Salvador. Most of the art depicts events in the lives of Romero and Grande.

Palm Frond illustration created by Spnr Cartman from the Noun Project. A palm frond is symbolic of Christian martyrdom.

Cover Design by Linda Wolf
Edited by Eric Wolf

ISBN 978-1-943901-04-3
Library of Congress Control Number: 2016942390

Published by Lectio Publishing, LLC
Hobe Sound, Florida 33455
www.lectiopublishing.com

In loving gratitude to my parents José and Matilde Pineda
for instilling in me the love of my cultural heritage

To Tío Flavio and Tía Lolita who shared with me
their love for Rutilio Grande

CONTENTS

ABBREVIATIONS

DOCUMENTS	
CEE	*Monseñor Romero: Cuadernos de Ejercicios Espirituales* (Bishop Romero: Notebooks of Spiritual Exercises)
ARCHIVES / LIBRARIES	
APCSJ	*Archivo de la Provincial Centroamericana de la Compañía de Jesús* (Archive of the Centroamerican Province of the Society of Jesus), San Salvador, El Salvador
BRP	De Paul University Special Collection: Brockman-Romero Papers, Chicago, IL
CCR	Archdiocesan Office for Canonization Cause for Monseñor Romero, San Salvador, El Salvador.
CMR	*Biblioteca de Teología, Centro Monseñor Romero,* Universidad Centroamericana (The Theology Library of the Bishop Romero Center, Central American University) San Salvador, El Salvador.
RTW	Romero Trust website, http://www.romerotrust.org.uk.

PREFACE

Close to four decades have passed since the murders of Rutilio Grande, S.J. (1977), and Archbishop Óscar Romero (1980) in El Salvador. With the passage of time, unfortunately, the stories of each man have become elusive and vague, especially for the generations who did not live through the turbulent years of the Salvadoran civil war. Persons who knew both men or were familiar with their contributions suggest that over this extended span of years, the images of the men have been aggrandized to the point of obscuring their humanity. In many ways, the ultimate discipleship of each man has become so idealized that while they inspire, they also remain beyond the imitation of ordinary men and women. This stalemate applies not only to Salvadorans but also to Christians outside of that small country who have heard the stories, particularly of Romero's martyrdom. Even fewer have motivating knowledge of Rutilio Grande, S.J. who was the first priest killed in El Salvador at the outset of the civil war. In fact, Grande is often only referred to as the friend of Romero who was murdered three weeks after the installation of Óscar Romero as Archbishop of San Salvador.

Nevertheless, on February 4, 2015, following a long process of consideration, Pope Francis's decision to beatify Archbishop Óscar Romero, martyr of El Salvador was announced by Archbishop Vincenzo Paglia, the Vatican official leading Romero's sainthood process. Decades after his death, however, Romero remained a controversial figure in the life of the Church and of the country of El Salvador. So for some, the news of his beatification was joyful, for others, troubling. But in the apostolic letter of beatification, Pope Francis declared: "Óscar Arnulfo Romero y Galdámez, Bishop and martyr, pastor according to the heart of Christ, evangelizer and father of the poor, heroic witness of the Kingdom of God, Kingdom of Justice, of fraternity, of peace."

Cardinal Amato characterized Romero's life as a "preparation for martyrdom," and underscored the significance of Father Rutilio

Grande in that journey. Earlier, Archbishop Paglia of the Vatican had also announced the initiation of the beatification process for Rutilio Grande, S.J. Furthermore, the Prefect's homily at Romero's beatification celebration concluded with the assertion that: "It is impossible to know Romero without knowing Rutilio Grande." That statement resonated with those who knew the story of Romero's persecution for his pastoral defense of the poor and vulnerable in El Salvador, a statement that notably incorporated Rutilio Grande's story as well.

The intent of this book is simple: to present these two men as models for those Christians seeking to deepen their own spiritual lives and to commit themselves to the pursuit of justice. It is important to underscore that this book is not a biography of either man. That task is left to others. In order to shed light on who they were as men and how they lived out their Christian commitment, this presentation of Bishop Romero and Rutilio Grande considers particularly human dimensions of their spiritual lives. In fact, the beauty of their examples lies in the fact that they were ordinary men, subject to diverse and sometimes contradictory life forces, struggling to live out their Christian vision.

To tell this story, I have drawn from years of research not only from various archives but also from listening to the stories told by men and women who knew Romero and Grande. Neither effort has been easy. Many of my interviewees, who had participated in that moment of history, have been warmly generous to me in returning to memories of an always deeply moving and often painful era in their lives. In some cases, it should be noted, access to certain archives has been restricted in an effort to avoid creating obstacles in the promotion of the canonization of Archbishop Romero. In other instances, there has been cautious reluctance to allow access to treasured collections.

As with everything in life, there is so much more that could be explored in the stories of these two Christian heroes of El Salvador. My hope, however, is that this glimpse into their lives will inspire and comfort those of us who struggle in our efforts to make this world a more just one.

This story also holds both professional and personal importance for me. As a child born in El Salvador, I migrated to the U.S. with my family when I was two years old. In my family of five children, we were fortunate that our parents kept memories of our home country alive. When I was a teenager, I returned to visit El Salvador for the first of what would become many subsequent trips. I gradually learned more and more about the country of my birth, and came to know my family members there.

While visiting relatives in the summer of 1976, I heard the name of Rutilio Grande, S.J. for the first time. My paternal aunt Lolita was married to his older brother, Flavio Grande, and as we sat in the living room, Tío Flavio showed me the family photo album and pointed to a photo of Rutilio, his younger brother. Flavio urged me to travel to Aguilares to meet Rutilio who was a parish priest there. Unfortunately though I tried, I was unable to meet my priest "uncle." When I returned the following summer, Rutilio Grande, S.J. was dead. He had been murdered on March 12, 1977.

Also during one of those family visits to El Salvador, I heard the name of Archbishop Óscar Romero for the first time. As was true of many Salvadoran families, my relatives had mixed views of the bishop. Emotions ran high in family conversations about him. For some he was a good man, and for others he was the source of all the difficulties that the country was experiencing.

One Sunday at the beach with my family, my uncle turned on the radio in time for Romero's Sunday sermon. As Romero spoke, my uncle vehemently criticized the sermon, increasing my curiosity about the controversial Archbishop. Consequently, one day I called the chancery office and scheduled a visit with him on August 17, 1979. I will never forget my visit with Archbishop Romero, or the quiet, self-possessed spirit of the man that sat opposite me. The meeting was memorable in itself, but I did not fully realize the personal significance of that encounter. A year later, from the back of the chapel of *La Divina Providencia*, a lone assassin fired a single shot to murder the Archbishop as he celebrated the Eucharist.

In 1980 when the outbreak of the civil war made it dangerous to travel, I suspended my visits to El Salvador. From California, however, I maintained contact with my family. When the civil war ended, I resumed my visits to El Salvador with a more informed understanding of what the country had suffered. My earlier interest in the life and legacy of Archbishop Romero revived and I pursued every opportunity to learn more about him, thus beginning my research. Later, through my relatives, I rediscovered Rutilio Grande, S.J. In the last decade, my research on each man has expanded as I searched in archives and conducted extended interviews with those who knew the men. I have also collected photos of murals depicting Romero and Grande that suggest not only a friendship between them, but their historical significance within El Salvador and beyond.

This book intends to tell a story of committed Christian lives and to inspire others to learn how to do the same. It has been a labor of love, made possible only with the support of countless friends, colleagues, community members and extended family. I owe a tremendous debt of gratitude to Monseñor Ricardo Urioste, Salvador Carranza, S.J., Rodolfo Cardenal, S.J., Robert Pelton, C.S.C., for their many contributions to the project of keeping the life and legacy of Archbishop Romero and Rutilio Grande, S.J., alive and for sharing that enthusiasm with me. I am deeply grateful to the University of Santa Clara for generously supporting me with the opportunity to craft this work. I am especially fortunate to have had the support of Jesuit colleagues and friends at Santa Clara University, Paul Crowley, S.J.; Luis Calero, S.J.; Dr. Juan Velasco, Lulu Santana and its President Michael Engh, S.J. Dr. Gary Macy, former chair of the religious studies department, has been one of my most enthusiastic supporters in this project. Father John Spain of Maryknoll has been a great resource in understanding the ecclesial history of El Salvador. Nor could I omit my thanks to Father Virgilio Elizondo and Dr. Timothy Matovina for their continuing encouragement and insight. As a professor, I am gratified to have the generous assistance of former students—Olga Pavisich-Ryan, Rosario Ballew and Alejandra Lizardo. I want to express my gratitude for the use of the De Paul University Special Collection (Brockman-Romero archives) in Chicago, Illinois, the *Archivo de la Provincial Centroamericana de la Compañía de Jesús* (Archive of the Central American Province of the Society of Jesus), *La Oficina Arquidiócesana para la Causa de Canonización de Monseñor Romero*, and the library at the *Centro Monseñor Romero* of the Central American University (UCA) in San Salvador, El Salvador.

I am particularly grateful for the sisterly affection and support of my community of the Institute of the Sisters of Mercy. I would be remiss in not giving special thanks to Genemarie Beegan, R.S.M. for her generous artistic and technical support. The love of my Pineda Escamilla and Grande Pineda family is a source of joy and sustenance for me. I am particularly blessed to count among them my brothers, Tony, Ernie, Roberto, and sisters Tita, Vilma, and their spouses and children. Finally, the sharing of ideas and editorial suggestions of Lourdes Thuesen enriches my writing. I owe a special expression of gratitude to Brennan Hill and Eric Wolf for believing in this project and encouraging its publication.

Ana María Pineda, R.S.M.
November 29, 2015

Since the writing of this preface, we have lost two persons who contributed valuable support and insight for this work. Monseñor Ricardo Urioste of El Salvador, who actively supported my interest and love of the legacy of Archbishop Romero and Father Rutilio Grande, died on January 15, 2016. In spite of his advanced age and many obligations, Monseñor Urioste not only made time to collaborate in my project, but also transcribed Romero's original reflection written on the death of his father, which is included as an Appendix to this publication.

Then, on March 14, 2016, the Hispanic ecclesial community in the U.S. lost their beloved pioneer theologian Father Virgilio Elizondo. For years he encouraged me to write and was delighted, not only when he heard that I was working on the legacy of Archbishop Romero and Father Grande, but especially so when the book was completed. While I mourn the passing of both of these men, I consider myself profoundly blessed to have had them in my life as mentors and friends.

AMP

Detail, photograph of Salvadoran mural. Murals expressing the life and influence of Archbishop Óscar Romero and Father Rutilio Grande can be found especially throughout Aguilares and El Paisnal in the Salvadoran Department of San Salvador.

CHAPTER 1

THE EARLY YEARS

El Salvador—a Pacific Rim land of lush and shady green, imposing volcanoes and flowing waters—like the other nations of Central America, experienced the twentieth century as a time of radical change and upheaval. The first half of the century saw a society clearly divided among an elite ruling class, an aspiring middle class, and a marginated laboring class of poor workers and farmers. Although—again like the other nations of the region—the history of El Salvador contained incidences of periodic changes of government, often by force, few anticipated the violent upheaval of the basic social structure experienced in the armed conflict between the classes, which irrupted in the second half of the century, carrying over an aftermath of instability into the new millennium.

This is the story of two men whose lives bridged the turbulent transformation of the country and left an indelible mark on the history of their beloved Church. Born ten years apart and having developed different personalities, they each chose a lifetime of ministry to the People of God in El Salvador. Although their personalities led them down different paths of service, their journeys show striking points of similarity in priestly lives that occasionally overlapped, and eventually were joined in the ultimate sacrifice of their lives in Christian martyrdom.

The figures of Monseñor Óscar Arnulfo Romero Galdámez and Rutilio Grande García, S.J., present compelling models not only of lives unfolding in a world of conflict and oppression, but also of personal spiritual journeys purified through failure and human weakness. Their cultural roots, their family influences, their spiritual struggles, their proximity to each other's life, and their fundamental humanness, provide a model of discipleship for all contemporary Christians.

Besides the socio-economic realities of El Salvador, both men's family structures and childhood experiences and challenges created the contexts from which they developed their gifts, spirituality, and vision.

Óscar Romero

Óscar Romero was born August 15, 1917, the third child of eight to Santos Romero and Guadalupe de Jesús Galdámez in Ciudad Barrios in the San Miguel Department of El Salvador. By the standards of the town, the Romero family was not poor. Nevertheless, his parents worked hard for their living. His father was a telegraph operator, and after hours tended a farm that his wife had inherited. The farm had several acres of coffee and a small cow that provided milk for the children. The farm yield made it possible for the family to make ends meet.[1] Doña Guadalupe worked at home caring for the large family. As the couple struggled financially, there were times when, despite their efforts, the family endured economic hardship.

Although Óscar's birth was uneventful, according to his younger brother Gaspar, their mother, Doña Guadalupe intuited early on that this child would one day surprise them.[2] How he would surprise them was never clarified, but perhaps Doña Guadalupe had noted intelligence in young Óscar that was already "surprising" his mother. Despite his normal birth, Óscar did not have a strong physical constitution as a child. At the age of five he became very ill with a debilitating fever that left him weak and paralyzed. Unable to move his legs and arms, he could not speak or feed himself or move freely. In order to get around, he dragged himself around the floor. While their parents worked, his sister, Zaída, who was about two years younger, was left to take care of Óscar. She became his nurse, attending to his needs. Over time however, the child relearned how to walk, speak, and feed himself.[3]

Since Óscar's illness was never diagnosed, however, it carried unfortunate consequences. The townspeople, uncertain of the origins of the child's malady, feared that their own children could be affected by the illness. Fearing that the illness could be contagious, the townspeople kept their children at a distance from the young boy, increasing Óscar's isolation. His interaction with his own family limited by their daily responsibilities, Óscar then experienced further isolation from other children. At a time when most of his peers were exploring the world around them and engaging in the normal childhood experiences, Óscar suffered under the burden of his own physical fragility.

According to his biographer, Jesús Delgado, the illness forced the boy into a solitude that shaped his personality. Understandably, he was a rather shy and timid boy. He was accustomed to his own company and that of his sister Zaída or the company of a select group of family members and friends. In later years, Romero's tendency would follow similar childhood patterns. He preferred to be alone, surrounding himself with a small circle of friends with whom he could truly feel comfortable. Outside of his circle, he came across to others as aloof, an outward manifestation of his inner insecurity and shyness.

During his illness, he had been showered by the constant care not only of his family, but also by solicitous neighbors. Unfortunately, Óscar came to expect such treatment. When he wasn't the center of attention, he turned irritable and cranky. In later years, his brothers would recall how Óscar sometimes woke up in the morning in a bad mood without being able to explain the reason for his feelings.

Jesús Delgado claimed that in many ways, Óscar exhibited some of his father's traits. The head of the family, Santos Romero had the reputation of being prone to outbursts of anger, which the children learned to endure. Unfortunately, this aspect of his father's character would carry into Óscar's adulthood; overcoming his angry and sometimes irritable disposition toward others became a lifelong undertaking. In his spiritual diary the developing Óscar often referenced his resolution to overcome this tendency to anger. Introspective in nature, he was most comfortable when alone; he found difficulty in interacting with large groups of people.

Once the boy had regained his health, he proved to be intellectually curious and enjoyed learning. However, he did not like attending the local school and sharing learning with classmates. He especially shied away from the girls. Despite his idiosyncrasies, Óscar was a good student. Jesús Delgado, recounts that Don Antonio de Cid, Óscar's teacher, remembered his student as serious and dedicated, intellectually engaged.[4] However, the town's school only provided three years of education, so his father arranged for Romero to continue his schooling with a local teacher, Anita Iglesias. Santos Romero took an active interest in his son's formation and education. When—away at school at the age of seventeen—Óscar received the news of his father's death, he gratefully recalled his father's loving efforts. In a reflection, Óscar wrote, "And of my youth, how can I not recall your concern for my formation? It is impossible to recall all of my memories, but they are alive in my memory and in my heart that blesses you."[5]

In the home, all the siblings had helped out with the family tasks, often assisting their father in delivering telegrams. Óscar also quickly learned how to actually send telegrams. He mastered the use of the telegraph machine and sometimes sent out messages. In addition, from his father he also learned carpentry techniques, and through his father's efforts he was apprenticed to Juan Leiva the owner of the local carpentry shop.[6] Skilled at carpentry, even as a young boy, Óscar made tables, chairs and doors. Some of his handiwork was kept in Ciudad Barrios and displayed in ongoing years.

His father also enjoyed music and played the flute, which he taught Óscar how to play. From boyhood Óscar had a love for music; besides the flute, in the seminary he learned how to play the piano. As an adult, although he listened to classical music, he favored the popular "marimba" music that he enjoyed while driving or during his quiet times at home. Also from his father who would spend many moments at home reading, Óscar developed his love for reading. These quiet times were respected by the children, and influenced Óscar's love for books.

Complementary to his solitary character, Óscar seemed internally drawn to prayer. The town's mayor, Alfonso Leiva, noted that the boy, after helping his father deliver telegrams, would take time to stop at church to pray and visit the saints. His brother Gaspar recalled that after school Óscar would stop by the parish church to visit the pastor, and help out by sweeping the church and assisting at mass.[7] Although Óscar's father often told him to stop bothering the local parish priest, Óscar continued his visits. His custom of seeking out time for prayer became an integral part of Romero's adult spirituality.

Santos played his flute at all the religious festivities, and the whole family joined their father in these processions and religious events. Óscar became imbued with the popular religiosity of the town. Inspired by these religious observances, Óscar would prepare his own processions.

Each year after Lent, Óscar, with the help of a select group of friends, prepared a procession to honor Saint Anthony. The task of adorning a chair with colored paper and framing the image of Saint Anthony with palms fell solely to Óscar and his male friends. He did not allow his sister Zaída or her friends to be involved in what he considered "men's" work. However, once the procession was ready, he expected Zaída and her friends to participate. His sister, Zaída, would decline and only after some pleading would she sometimes agree to participate in Óscar's religious activity. At the end of the procession, Óscar climbed on top of a pile of rocks and delivered a sermon. This occurred each year.

Óscar's call to the priesthood came when he was thirteen years old. The town's mayor, Alfonso Leiva, had noted the young Romero's devotion to the Church and had often observed the boy's daily visits to the parish. When the first bishop of San Miguel, Juan Antonio Dueñas y Argumedo came to town on a pastoral visit, the mayor mentioned to the Bishop that he thought that Óscar Romero had a vocation to the priesthood. This observation led to the initial encounter between the Bishop and Óscar.[8]

Bishop Dueñas y Argumedo's visit caused great excitement in the town. Óscar pleaded with his mother to dress him up in his finest clothes. He wanted to greet the bishop and wanted to look his best. His mother dressed him in a fine white suit and a hat. The boy did catch the attention of the prelate, and Óscar was invited to accompany the Bishop on all his rounds. That encounter and moment was indelibly imprinted on Romero's mind and heart. Years later, in an account written by María Vigil, Romero recounted how the bishop called to him in front of the crowd of townspeople and asked him what he wanted to be. Óscar replied that he wanted to be a priest. With that, the bishop raised his finger and pointed it straight at Óscar's forehead, announcing that Óscar was going to be a bishop. Fifty years later, Monseñor Romero touched that place on his forehead and told María Vigil, "I can still feel the touch of his finger right here."[9]

The following year Romero left Ciudad Barrios to pursue his desire to become a priest, entering the minor seminary in San Miguel. The seminary formation program was in the hands of the Claretian Order. The community's devotion to Mary, the mother of God, and to the Blessed Sacrament was an integral part of their seminary formation. Since Romero had been born on the feast of the Assumption of Mary, his mother believed that her son was under the special protection of Mary. Now, in addition to the Marian devotion nurtured in his family, the Claretians' devotion to Mary and the Blessed Sacrament would shape Romero's personal spirituality and carry over into his adulthood. Having been a good student and upon completion of his studies with the Claretians, Romero took the next step in his journey to the priesthood and entered the major seminary of San José de la Montaña in San Salvador.

As was customary, during Romero's seminary years his family was expected to provide for their son with all personal items including clothes. Although Romero's family was not considered poor, this obligation was a financial burden for his parents. Óscar's father and mother struggled to find ways to cover the cost of having their son in the seminary. One of the gifts that Romero would take with him to the seminary was a beautiful silver-plated flute from his father. As his father had taught him how to play the flute, the instrument was a fitting gift for his son.

Besides his ability to play the flute, Romero arrived at the seminary with several skills that he had acquired during his youth and for which he would find good use. In the telegraph office alongside his father, he had learned how to type, and he could also write basic musical notations. In the seminary, his creative ability with music would earn him the nickname of "the boy with the flute—*el niño de la flauta.*"

From the time of his early childhood, Romero demonstrated leadership qualities. It has been noted that despite his childhood illness that had kept him away from interacting with his peers, with the help of a small circle of friends Romero had managed to organize an annual procession for St. Anthony. In the minor seminary, he used his typing and musical skills at the service of his classmates, few of whom could do either. Romero subsequently found himself in the enviable position of being able to type for the seminary newsletter; he also composed musical pieces that were used in the seminary for special events.

Óscar honed his declamatory skills alongside his classmate, Rafael Valladares. Competing with each other, they recited poems and other literary pieces, taking turns at being awarded first place. In this early activity, Romero showed promising signs of becoming a gifted public speaker.

Rutilio Grande

Ten years after Óscar Romero was born and was developing through his childhood, Rutilio Grande came into the world on July 5, 1928 in El Paisnal—one of the poorest little towns in the San Salvador department of El Salvador. Although Rutilio's birth was normal, he was not a strong child. The youngest of six sons born to Salvador Grande and Cristina García, his father Salvador owned a town store that functioned as a gathering place for the townspeople. Unfortunately, the store did little to provide for the family's basic needs. His parents struggled to raise their children.

When Rutilio was about three or four years old, the situation at home worsened. After a serious marital disagreement, Rutilio's parents separated. His father left for Honduras leaving the family under the care of their mother Cristina. Unable to sustain themselves economically, the family fell into abject poverty. Soon afterwards, Rutilio's mother died leaving the children in the care of their paternal grandmother Francisca. Eventually Don Salvador was forced to return home to take care of the family.

With their mother dead and their father absent, Rutilio's brothers struggled to make a living. The eldest brother Flavio rented a couple of acres of land at some distance from El Paisnal. Every morning, led by Flavio, the brothers left to work the land while young Rutilio stayed at home with his grandmother Francisca. She prepared the noon meal for the brothers, and Rutilio would hoist the hot pot of food, climb onto a donkey, and take it to his brothers. Once he was there, the young Rutilio served his brothers their lunch. At home, he tended the pigs and helped out with other household tasks. Life in the Grande household was difficult but all the brothers found ways to contribute. At night, his grandmother prepared dinner and the family would share one plate of food from which they all ate. Upon his grandmother's death, Rutilio recalled those difficult but cherished moments. He wrote: "She who would for many years be the one to prepare our meals when we would sit at the table with our father to eat from the same plate…and the one who would prepare food that I would take to the "boys" as she would often say."[10]

After his brother Flavio married, his wife, María Lola (Lolita) Grande Pineda helped with the care of the Grande brothers. Even though Lolita, as she was called, was just in her teens, she became responsible for washing and ironing all the Grande brothers' clothing. As their paternal grandmother Francisca aged, Lolita began to share the responsibility for preparing meals for the Grande brothers. Lolita also found herself giving special maternal care to Rutilio who was the youngest and was in most need of her attention.

As Lolita later recounted, Rutilio clung to her, seeking the affection of a mother. One of the stories that Lolita told was how when she first began to care for Rutilio, she washed a night shirt that he clung to but which needed washing. For days he asked for it despite the fact that it had been replaced by a freshly laundered one. Finally, Lolita had to tell him that a "little mouse had taken it away." That seemed to settle the question but he was unhappy about it. In her recollection, Rutilio was a serious and well-behaved child. He had a pleasant manner, yet had a serious air about him even into his adulthood. As a child, he liked to both play ball and tell jokes.[11]

The entire family was living a difficult reality. There were days when all they had to eat were tortillas with a pinch of salt.[12] While all were affected by these difficult times, it may have had a particularly severe impact on the young Rutilio who also lived the trauma of his parents' separation and his mother's death. His family's economic and emotional upheavals while Rutilio was quite young seem to have had a long-lasting effect on his health and psychological well-being.

As a child Rutilio had a delicate temperament. He became upset easily and avoided others. When left to his own preference, he kept to his grandmother Francisca's company most of the day, clinging to her and hanging onto her skirt. Francisca, however, taught him his prayers. She devoted many hours to the care of the altar in the town's church and Rutilio always accompanied her. He therefore became familiar with the church's liturgical celebrations, its vestments and sacred vessels. This childhood familiarity with the liturgical aspect of Church life would, in fact, become part not only of his studies but, later, the focus of his ministerial interest. Throughout his vocational life, he was known for giving significant time and attention to the preparation of liturgical events.

Family members recalled how as a little boy, Rutilio organized a daily "mass" over which he presided. For vestments he placed a shirt or a cape on his shoulders. He enlisted his older cousins and their friends to set up an altar table beneath a large *carao* fruit tree. The children's tasks included sweeping the floor and covering the altar table with a table cloth. The seed of the *carao* tree was round and resembled the shape of the host. At the moment when Rutilio elevated the "host," one of his assistants rang a small set of bells that belonged to Rutilio. Then he gave the fruit tree seeds as "communion" to his assistants. When the bells rang everyone in the small town of El Paisnal knew that "Rutilio's Mass" was being celebrated.[13]

Acquaintance with a parish priest or bishop seemed to be the most common way that young boys in El Salvador found their calling to the priesthood. Rutilio's call to the priesthood came in a manner interestingly similar to Romero's experience. When Rutilio was thirteen years old, Luis Chávez y González, the Archbishop of San Salvador, came to El Paisnal for a Confirmation ceremony. The archbishop was only thirty-nine years old and one of the youngest to be ordained. Rutilio was called upon to accompany the archbishop to the surrounding towns.

Soon after the archbishop left El Paisnal, Rutilio wrote to him expressing a desire to enter the seminary of San José de la Montaña in San Salvador. On behalf of the archbishop, the rector of the seminary in San Salvador responded expressing the archbishop's desire to have Rutilio enter the seminary. The letter also indicated the economic obligations that Rutilio's family would need to assume. It is clear from the exchange of letters that the Grande family was unable to assume full payment. Archbishop Chávez y González, therefore, agreed to pay for Rutilio's seminary tuition, while the family would be responsible for all living expenses there. To cover the expenses for their little brother, his brothers eventually sold some of their livestock.

Rutilio and the thirty-nine-year-old archbishop maintained a life-long correspondence that Rutilio treasured and saved. After Rutilio's death, among his belongings was found a well-kept file that contained all the correspondence that he had received from the archbishop for over thirty-six years. The collection included that first letter Archbishop Luis Chávez y González had sent to Rutilio. The letter was dated May 12, 1940.

> My very dear Rutilio,
>
> I received the affectionate letter you sent me…it pleased me so much that you wrote to me and I hope that it will not be the last time. Today is the feast of Pentecost, the day when the church celebrates the coming of the Holy Spirit…ask the Holy Spirit …that if it is his pleasure, your holy desires of becoming a priest should be realized.
>
> Try during this year not to lose any class days, and to pay attention to reading, writing, arithmetic and grammar; tell the Director of the School, on my behalf, that he give you special classes in arithmetic and grammar, …that they teach you well the four rules and, if it is possible, the concepts of fractions and decimals, and also that they teach you how to conjugate verbs…[14]

As is evident in the tone of that initial correspondence, from the beginning the archbishop treated Rutilio like a son. Throughout the years, the archbishop continued to offer Rutilio his loving advice. Rutilio considered Archbishop Chávez y González the father of his vocation to the priesthood. In later years, Rutilio often made reference to his childhood encounter with the bishop and how it awakened his vocation to the priesthood. In December of 1974, on the occasion of

Archbishop Chávez y González' fifty-year anniversary to the priesthood, Rutilio wrote: "You passed by on my life's path when you were a young Archbishop and I just a child of thirteen years old…After God I owe my vocation to you as a visible instrument of God's grace. It is through you that God chose to call me explicitly to this vocation of service in the Church…"[15]

Rutilio's life journey had started in the tiny town of El Paisnal but the road ahead could not have been imagined by this timid and fragile young boy.

Although Romero and Grande were both from families grounded in the reality of El Salvador, their early challenges were different. Romero had to deal with the onset of illness at an early age, yet with the support of an intact, solicitous family. Grande, on the other hand, had to learn to deal with family tensions brought on by the effects of rural subsistence and the breakup of the family unit. The effects of their respective difficult experiences in their early life would come to mark their later years.

Romero and Rutilio's youthful interests and experiences took shape within the context of their families and hometowns. Romero's participation in his father's job at the town's telegraph office introduced him to the importance of communication. Rutilio's daily exposure to the care of the town's church gave him a love for the ceremonies of worship. As boys, both of them were familiar with and drawn to the popular practices of piety, thus fostering their nascent relationships with God. Attentive to God's presence, each was being prepared for future moments of grace and call.

ENDNOTES

1. Jesús Delgado, *Monseñor, Pro-manucrito*, (BRP). See Delgado, *Óscar A. Romero Biografía*, 2005.
2. Interview with Gaspar Romero, March 9, 2010.

3. Delgado, *Monseñor, Pro-manucrito*, 6. See Delgado, *Romero Biografía*.

4. Martin Maier, *Monseñor Romero: Maestro de Espiritualidad*, 27.

5. Ibid., 25. Spanish citation: "*¿Y mi juventud ?no recuerda tu esfuerzo por mi formación? Imposible recorrer todos los recuerdos, pero aquí están vivos en mi memoria y en mi corazón que te bendice.*"

6. *Revista Cultural* No. 114, Enero-Marzo 2015, 27.

7. Ibid., 16.

8. A more detailed account of Romero's call to the priesthood can be found in "*Testimonio de Tiberio Arnoldo Romero, hermano de Monseñor Óscar Arnulfo Romero*" account in *Revista Cultural* No. 114, Enero-Marzo 2015, 27-28.

9. Maria López Vigil, *Monseñor Romero: Memories in Mosaic*, 16.

10. Letter from Rutilio Grande to Flavio Grande, April 3, 1963 (APCSJ). Spanish citation: "*Ella, la que nos preparó la comida durante mucho tiempo cuando nos sentábamos a la mesa con nuestro padre para comer de un mismo plato en la casa solariega, y la que preparaba aquellos 'bastamientos' que yo trasportaba y llevaba a los 'muchachos' como ella solía decir.*"

11. Interview with María Lola Grande Pineda, May 4, 2014.

12. Interview with Alirio Grande Pineda, May 4, 2014.

13. Interview with María Lola Grande Pineda, May 4, 2014. Spanish citation: "*La misa de Rutilio.*"

14. Letter from Archbishop Chávez y González to Rutilio Grande, May 12, 1940 (APCSJ).

15. Letter from Rutilio Grande to Archbishop Chávez y González, December 1974 (APCSJ). Spanish citation: "*Pasó Usted junto al camino de mí vida cuando era un joven Arzobispo y yo apenas un niño de 13 años...Despúes de Dios a Usted le debo mí vocación como instrumento visible de las gracias del Señor: Por medio de Usted quiso llamarme explícitamente Aquél que me había escogido para esta vocación de servicio en su Iglesia.*"

Detail, photograph of altar mural in the church at El Paisnal where Padre Rutilio Grande is buried. The mural, depicting Óscar Romero and Rutilio Grande con-celebrating mass, was removed in 2013.

CHAPTER 2

PRIESTLY CALL AND FORMATION

The U.S. Stock Market crash of Wall Street in 1929 had severe repercussions for El Salvador. The Salvadoran coffee market, which depended on the U.S. economy, was devastated. To generate some profit, frantic landowners attempted to decrease workers' meager salaries, thereby intensifying the destitution of the poor in El Salvador. Tensions between peasants and land-owning elites escalated. The 1932 peasant uprising in El Salvador protested the abuses of the landowners and consequently incited brutal government retaliation often referred to as "*La Matanza*" or "The Slaughter." Approximately 40,000 indigenous people and political opponents were murdered, imprisoned, or exiled. The following years saw a succession of authoritarian governments. To maintain power, the regimes limited any type of reform and used severe political repression to control the people.

The close of WWII brought on a tremendous change in the geopolitical balance and worldwide economy; as a result of global war, entire nations had to recover and rebuild. It was a time of challenges and radical dynamics. For the Catholic Church, global upheaval became the impetus for stringent self-examination and renewal. In 1962, under the leadership of the post-war Pontiff, Pope Saint John XXIII, the Second Vatican Council was convened. As a major document announced: the Church was to reappraise itself in the context of the modern world. One of the goals was to bring the liturgy into relevance with the lives of twentieth-century Catholics, and to explicitly acknowledge the laity as active participants in Church life. With these objectives, the Council unleashed a dynamic of fresh thinking and prompted the appearance of international centers devoted to the cultures, vocation, and education of the laity.

On the brink of this upheaval, Óscar Romero had finished his studies and was engaged in pastoral work. Rutilio Grande, on the other hand, was in the early stages of the process that would form him for his priesthood.

Óscar Romero

Óscar Romero's call to the priesthood unfolded during this turbulent time in the political life of El Salvador.

In 1930, Romero at the age of 13 left home to enter the minor seminary of San Miguel. Archbishop Juan Antonio Dueñas y Argumedo of San Miguel was a man with a love for education. He was extremely well read and known for his linguistic skills, and had taken great care in placing the seminary in the hands of the Claretian priests. The Claretians were highly versed in the art of teaching rhetoric, in cultivating fine manners and in nurturing piety in their seminarians. Consequently, the seminary had an exceptional reputation as a place of fine learning.

San Miguel provided an excellent context for the young Romero who in his childhood was known not only for his piety but also for his oratorical talent. Even as a child he recited poetry with great emotion and sentiment and was always sought out to recite poems for special occasions in Ciudad Barrios or at school. Although by nature rather introverted and shy, Óscar never declined an invitation to recite a poem in public.[1] The minor seminary of San Miguel aptly nurtured his interests and burgeoning talents. It was here, too, that he established a friendship with Rafael Valladares, which would span three decades until Valladares' death in 1961.

Besides the silver flute, Romero also took to the seminary a small typing machine that he had used at home. At San Miguel, with the material prepared by Valladares, Romero began to type the weekly seminary newsletter. Eventually he secured the use of a larger seminary typewriter. His involvements in the seminary life helped him not only to feel part of the group, but also to gain more expertise in the art of communication.

During his minor seminary years, encouraged by his talented classmate, Valladares, Romero honed his rhetorical abilities. He saved a notebook dated February 1, 1932 in which he kept his writing exercises.[2] Among the exercises, Romero included a draft of a letter that he was writing to his mother in which he experimented with turns of phrases and writing style. By the time that he completed his seminary studies in San Miguel, Romero had distinguished himself in not only reciting poems but also writing them.

The seminary's daily schedule set aside three times for prayer and left the rest of the day to classes including time for rest and recreation. One of the favored recreational activities for the seminarians was field trips to the countryside and nearby volcanoes. In general, the seminary formation fostered not only a sense of community among the young men but also an appreciation for humor,[3] an environment that was cherished by Romero. In terms of spiritual development, the Claretians imbued the seminary with special devotion to both Mary, the Mother of God, and the Blessed Sacrament, emphases that would characterize the spirituality of the maturing Romero.

In 1937, Romero entered the major seminary of San José de la Montaña. Later that year his father Santos Romero died; the young seminarian received the news of his father's death on August 14, 1937. In a moving reflection, he expressed his profound grief:

> "My Papá has died! Papá, every afternoon I directed my gaze toward the far off east, sending you from a distance my loving remembrance. I could see you in the hallway of my well-remembered home, leaning against the blue hand railing, I could see you gazing at the sunset in your son's direction …I remember that once I heard you say: 'the place where the sun sets..! Oh, those of us who have already declined westward!" And, now, father, who answers to my filial gaze? My mother, oh yes, my mother! But, you, my beloved father? Oh! I no longer gaze on you living…[4]

Romero studied at the major seminary in San Salvador for only a short time. On September 22, 1937, after receiving the tonsure marking his progress toward priesthood, he was sent to Rome for doctoral studies. His years in Rome coincided with World War II. In 1962, looking back to those years, Romero wrote:

> "Europe and almost the whole world were a conflagration during the Second World War. Fear, uncertainty, news of bloodshed made for an environment

> of dread. At the Latin American College rations grew smaller by the day…Hunger forced several Italian seminaries to close. The Latin American College had to cope with the situation, since all of its students were foreigners away from home; those who could return to their homelands took their chances in doing so. Those who stayed suffered more than ever from the separation. Almost every night sirens warned of enemy planes and one had to run for the shelters; twice they were more than an alarm and Rome's outskirts were scarred by horrible bombings."[5]

The austere reality of the war severely impacted the life in the house of studies. Food was often scarce and the seminarians lived on whatever the rector could procure. Romero also saw firsthand the dire situation of the ordinary people. One day as he made his way through the streets of Rome, he encountered a man who was begging for food. The gaunt image of the man disturbed Romero deeply. Upon returning to the house of studies, Romero went to the kitchen and, against the house rules related to the scarcity of supply that was available to the seminarians, took food and gave it to the poor beggar. Although a man of strict adherence to the rules, in this particular instance, Romero considered the stranger's need more important than the rules. The tensions of the war made it difficult for students to concentrate on their work. During these years of material deprivation, Romero learned to live with little, a habit that became part of his priestly life.

While studying in Rome, Romero specialized in ascetical theology, choosing to write his thesis on ascetics and mysticism. A perfectionist, Óscar continually worked and re-worked his thesis; but with the circumstances of war and the distractions that besieged all the seminarians, Romero never completed it. None of these difficulties, however, interfered with the development of his priestly spirituality. In a short article that he wrote in 1940, he summarized the essence of his priestly aspirations: "To be a crucified one with Christ who redeems. To be one with the Resurrected Christ who shares resurrection and life."[6]

Several of his biographers[7] have noted Romero's lifelong tendency to consider himself as unworthy and limited by human weaknesses. His persistent feelings of unworthiness exacerbated his tendencies toward scrupulosity, timidity and shyness. Looking to the crucified Christ, Romero found meaningful identification not only with the suffering Christ Crucified, but also with suffering humanity. He believed that without love, suffering was an empty experience, that the cross was redemptive only when totally embraced by love. From formative experiences, he realized that to understand God, it was important to understand the reality of people's lives. Early in his seminary years, understanding humanity, and especially suffering humanity, took on a spiritual imperative for Romero. Those strife-ridden yet rich years in the seminary in Rome came to be a lifelong source of inspiration for Romero and a touchstone of the deep spiritual fervor of his youth.

On April 4, 1942, while World War II continued to ravage Europe, Romero was ordained in the chapel of the Latin American College in Rome; in 1943, he embarked for El Salvador. The ship carried Romero and Father Valladares, his priest companion and friend, as far as Barcelona where they spent a few days. The ship that they took for the final part of the journey to Latin America stopped in Cuba. Because of Italy's association with Hitler through Mussolini, the Cuban government detained the passengers, checking their identities and motives for travel. Subsequently Romero and his companion were transported to a Cuban concentration camp. There they were required to perform menial tasks that, though familiar to them, proved to be demanding and exhausting. The deprivations of the camp, mainly the lack of adequate rest and nutrition, negatively affected their health. In December of 1943, after four months of detention, Redemptorist priests in Havana found out about their imprisonment and were able to secure the release of the two young priests.[8]

Leaving Cuba, they arrived in San Miguel on December 24, 1943, and were given a hero's welcome. During a great feast prepared to celebrate their safe homecoming, Romero requested that special attention be given to the poor of the town.[9] This was an early demonstration of his concern for the poor, which would deepen throughout his life.[10]

Shortly after his return to El Salvador, Romero was assigned to a parish in the small town of Anamorós; this assignment marked the beginning of his pastoral activity. Although his years of priestly formation had accentuated the world of books and academic study, that focus was about to change.

Rutilio Grande

On January 31, 1941, thirteen-year-old Rutilio left the small village of El Paisnal for the seminary of San José de La Montaña in San Salvador. The move to the capital was a great change for a young boy who had grown up in a small rural town.

Although his desire to become a priest dominated his vision of his future, his journey to the seminary stumbled over many obstacles. In an early letter to Luis Chávez y González, Archbishop of San Salvador, Rutilio wrote that his hope to enter the seminary was diminishing. Responding to the boy's letter, the Archbishop acknowledged the economic challenges and difficulties that entrance to the seminary posed for Rutilio's family. In a letter dated December 9, 1940, Fr. Agustín Bariáin, S.J.—rector of the seminary—responded to Rutilio's interest and explored the obstacles the boy faced.

> "My dear little friend: The Archbishop has informed me of your desire to enter the seminary, but despite your good intentions, you have no small measure of difficulties. Knowing this I hasten to plead with you that you come here to the seminary of San José de la Montaña, as soon as possible so that we can examine you and see how we can resolve these difficulties…"[11]

Rutilio's father's recent ill health compounded the financial demands made on the Grande family. Nevertheless, in a letter of October 19, 1940, the Archbishop encouraged Rutilio not to let his hopes wither, and asked him to hasten to visit him soon. He suggested that Rutilio ask his godfather, Facundo Barrera, for help in buying shoes, clothing, and other necessities. While Barrera did help with some of the clothing needs, Rutilio's older brother Flavio sold some of his livestock to cover other of his brother's expenses. Archbishop Chávez y González, for his part, assumed responsibility for the seminary tuition. In this collaboration of support, Rutilio was able to enter the seminary and begin his journey to the priesthood.

Rutilio arrived at the seminary as a boy coming from a small village with few educational opportunities. Although his grades had been average,[12] his academic effort was a solid indicator of what he could achieve with opportunity. There is no clear evidence of the nature of his piety as a seminarian but given the times, it is legitimate to imagine that it favored the traditional religious practices that he had been accustomed to in El Paisnal. He was also given responsibilities in several areas of seminary life, including, by 1944-45, the supervision of the dorms and of the seminary choir. In general, it appeared that Rutilio adapted to life in the seminary.

When Rutilio entered the seminary San José de la Montaña in San Salvador, it was administered by the Jesuits. The Central American province of *La Compañía de Jesús* (the Society of Jesus) had been established by Jesuits from Spain, and consequently, was heavily influenced by them. Exposed to the Jesuit spirituality and education, it is easy to understand that Rutilio developed an interest in them. Consequently, before completing the minor seminary, Rutilio expressed his desire to enter the Society of Jesus. In a letter of September 24, 1947, he also articulates his interest in missionary work, another possible rationale for entering the Society of Jesus.[13]

Before he formally requested admittance to the Jesuits, Rutilio informed Archbishop Chávez y González of his decision to leave the diocesan seminary. It must have been a disappointment for the Archbishop who had accompanied the young man in his initial calling and had placed such future hopes in him. Yet the archbishop responded generously indicating that the most important thing was to do God's will. After obtaining written permission from his father, Salvador Grande, Rutilio entered the Society of Jesus on September 5, 1945. He was one of the few native vocations at the time. Archbishop Chávez y González' affection for Rutilio, however, remained constant. In their correspondence the archbishop counseled him on how to nurture his priestly vocation. In a letter to Rutilio dated June 3, 1947, the archbishop wrote: "In order to maintain your holy vocation, your principal obligation is centered in always nourishing the ideal of becoming a priest, with God's grace and the protection of the Holy Blessed Virgin Mary."[14]

Throughout his life, Rutilio maintained a close relationship with the archbishop, often seeking his mentor's advice and sharing with him his spiritual and priestly journey.

Before taking first vows in the Society of Jesus on September 24, 1947, Rutilio expressed his desire to be sent to the Missions in China. In a letter written to Alvaro Echarri, S.J., on August 15, 1947, the feast of the Assumption of Mary, Rutilio wrote: "For some time, I have been thinking of this and I now want to express it to you: Since the days when I was in the seminary, I was attracted to a missionary vocation; Father, I know what it signifies, and it was one of the reasons that I was moved to enter the Company, with the hope of some day becoming a missionary to the infidels."[15]

The tone of the letter captures Rutilio's youthful fervor, his wish to give himself over to God fully. His letter concedes that a missionary life requires complete abnegation and true heroism. If God would grant him this desire, Rutilio would consider himself truly happy. Writing back on September 17, 1947, Fr. Echarri acknowledged Rutilio's letter and encouraged the young aspirant to live the virtue of sacred indifference which will lead him to embrace a life of prayer and union with God, mortification, purity, all virtues that are necessary for a missionary. In his conclusion, Echarri assured Rutilio that only God decides the future, a prediction that would fulfill itself in ways that Rutilio could not have anticipated.[16]

On September 24, 1947, the Feast of Our Lady of Mercy, Rutilio made his first vows in the Society of Jesus. The years that followed took Rutilio to Quito and Spain[17] as he pursued completion of his studies. In 1950, Rutilio was sent to Panama where he experienced his dark night of the soul. Shortly after his April arrival, sometime between mid-May and June, he suffered what was considered a severe psychotic episode. He was found unresponsive, unable to interact with those speaking to him or with the reality around him. According to Rodolfo Cardenal, a Spanish psychiatrist diagnosed the young Jesuit with catatonic schizophrenia and gave him a 60% chance of recovery.[18]

Although the Jesuit superiors sought medical programs that could help Rutilio recover, they found none in San Salvador. They decided to leave him in Panama where, fortunately, he responded well to intensive treatment. How long he remained in Panama is unclear. Eventually, however, he returned to the Jesuit residence in Santa Tecla, San Salvador, which he found restrictive.

By July 1951, Rutilio was assigned to the minor seminary of San José de la Montaña in San Salvador where he had begun his own studies. The change proved to be a good one for Rutilio. In a letter written to the Jesuit Vice-provincial dated July 8, 1951, Rutilio wrote: "Thanks be to God, I am improving. This robustness that I have regained since my experience in Panama, helps me, as I experience it in every regard."[19]

Life in the seminary, busy with inspections, classes, and dealing with the seminarians supported his ongoing recovery. He writes: "…as I have noted all this helps me greatly even for my health, as I have noticed since I left Santa Tecla to come to the Seminary."[20] He delighted in seminary work and in the interaction with the seminarians. In a letter to the Vice-provincial, he admitted that "it helps me with my somewhat introverted character."[21]

Yet Rutilio realized that he had to take care of himself by "eating well and taking a daily siesta, because the experience has taught me that I have to maintain great tranquility and avoid nervousness and extremes, even in the daily tasks."[22] In that letter, he reiterates several times how positive and even consoling it is for him to work with the seminarians. From 1951-53, Rutilio's responsibilities at the minor seminary included serving as sub-prefect of discipline as well as teaching Latin, Spanish, geography of El Salvador, and history of Central America.[23]

The cause of his severe illness was never really discovered. The medical records are non-existent. His biographer, Rodolfo Cardenal, S.J., suggests that it may have been brought about by the poverty and family disintegration that Rutilio had experienced in his childhood. Whatever the roots of that severe psychological break, the fact remains that for the rest of his life, Rutilio would suffer from bouts with depression and scrupulosity. Those few years serving in the minor seminary of San José de la Montaña in San Salvador, however, brought him needed healing. Furthermore, that experience at the seminary also awakened in him a love for future seminary formation.

In 1953, Rutilio was sent to Oña in Spain to begin his requisite studies in philosophy. During the year, Rutilio maintained correspondence with his Vice-provincial, Agustín Bariáin, periodically reporting on his experiences. In December 4, 1955, Rutilio wrote to Bariáin informing him that he had traveled to Bilbao to meet with Dr. González Pinto, a psychiatrist. Rutilio happily reported that González Pinto had examined him carefully for an hour and a quarter and had told him: "that I could be completely tranquil. Internally, I had been telling myself the same for quite some time."[24]

Being realistic, Rutilio acknowledged that he could no longer study as intensely as he did before. His schedule in Oña was demanding, the details of which he shared with his older brother Flavio with whom he maintained regular correspondence: "We get up at 6:00 in the morning... This is followed by an hour of prayer and Mass in order to begin the day in a saintly manner. Breakfast at 8:15 so that we can later give ourselves over to study which is our primary obligation so that we can be formed wisely for God's glory."[25] The morning included two hours of personal study time followed by two classes of fifty minutes each with lunch served at 1:00. Afterwards, the seminarians had 45 minutes of recreation and an equal amount of time for a nap. The afternoon included two classes of 50 minutes each, followed by 30 minutes of recreation at 5:30. The students then continued with two and a half hours of personal study time. Dinner was served at 9:00 p.m. with another 45 minutes of recreation. After 30 minutes of personal devotion, all the seminarians retired at 11:00 p.m.[26]

Given the demands of the daily schedule and routine, Rutilio understood that he had to pace himself to avoid unnecessary stress. In a letter of December 4, 1955, he wrote that he found it helpful to go out to the countryside and mountains and to methodically exercise every morning. The coolness of the mountain air invigorated him and stimulated his appetite. For him, these precautions were a small cross to bear, and everyday he ardently asked God for the gift of good health. Of course, he acknowledged that his own efforts were necessary in bringing this about.

Despite Oña's relative geographical isolation, it was a good place for Rutilio, a place where he grew physically healthier and relied upon prayer to fulfill his responsibilities, a pattern essential to his reflection and decision-making. While Oña promoted the recovery of his physical strength and health, it is also where he began catechetical work with the town's people. Giving religious instruction to the families and youth,[27] Rutilio demonstrated a natural gift for imparting religious instruction in a way that reached the people. While his talent for addressing the people from within their particular reality emerged in Oña, it manifested itself later in his ministry with other diverse populations.

In part, the genius of his work stemmed from pride in his own cultural roots. In the seminary, he was immersed in a cultural ethos highly influenced by Spain, and Rutilio would often say that he considered himself "like coffee with milk."[28] That is to say that he was a *mestizo*, a man of both Indigenous and Spanish blood. This in itself reflected not only pride in himself, but also the insight to honor the *mestizo* reality of Salvadorans. Throughout the rest of his life, his posture of cultural identification and sensitivity won the affection of the people to whom he ministered. Oña was no exception.

In the Monastery of Oña Rutilio was ordained to the priesthood on July 30, 1959. Even with the distance, Archbishop Chávez y González through their correspondence had accompanied Rutilio. In a letter written just days before his protégé's ordination, the archbishop wrote: "With an affectionate and loving greeting I send you this letter on the eve of your priestly ordination; my personal prayers go with it so that God, Our Lord and the Most Holy Virgin Mary keep you and protect you in your priesthood since without the grace of God and the assistance of the Blessed Mother, we can do little in such a sublime and incomparable state of the priesthood."[29] Many of the families from Oña with whom Rutilio had shared his life accompanied him in the event that was celebrated by the whole town. Although his own family was unable to attend, they celebrated the event in his native town (*tierra natal*) of El Paisnal.

In the midst of such apparent happiness, however, Rutilio suffered a profound anguish. In the pair of days between his diaconate and priestly ordination, Rutilio experienced a second psychological crisis. Overwhelmed with scrupulosity, he doubted whether he had correctly followed the formula in the diaconate ceremony, thereby invalidating it. The morning of his ordination to the priesthood, Rutilio sought out Marcelino Zalba, S.J., his spiritual advisor; unable to find him, Rutilio went ahead with his ordination. Burdened by his doubts, Rutilio subsequently shared his fears with Father Zalba who reassured him that his ordination was valid. Zalba even tore up Rutilio's copy of the vow formula that had caused the uncertainty. For the moment, all seemed to have been resolved.

Even a few years later however, an agonizing Rutilio continued to doubt the validity of his ordination. Unknown to Marcelino Zalba, the young priest had kept a copy of the supposedly problematic vow formula. Repeatedly he revisited the morning of his diaconate ordination. Rutilio read and re-read the vow formula that in his uncertainty he had changed slightly. After this lapse of several years, Rutilio wrote out several versions of his explanation and sent them on to Zalba in several separate mailings. Father Zalba responded assuring him of the legitimacy of his priesthood.[30] For the moment, Rutilio was reassured and his scruples alleviated. But the bout with scruples depleted him emotionally and his doubts did not dissolve completely. Finally, in August 1962, he determined to put his doubts behind him, and he tore up his copy of the questionable vow formula.[31]

In July 1960, Rutilio had completed his studies in philosophy and theology in Oña and returned to El Salvador. Assigned to the minor seminary, he taught Latin and the History of Central America and served as Prefect of Discipline from 1960-62. In 1963 he entered into the third stage of probation required in Jesuit formation (Tertianship) in Cordova, Spain, afterwards studying for a year at the Pastoral Institute of Lumen Vitae (1963-64) in Brussels. When he returned in 1965 to El Salvador, he assumed ministerial responsibilities at the minor seminary of San José de La Montaña as prefect of discipline, professor of pastoral theology and Director of pastoral work, and made his final vows in the Society of Jesus on August 15, 1972. With his studies complete, and as an ordained priest and vowed Jesuit,

Rutilio was poised for the flourishing of his exceptional ministerial talents.

ENDNOTES

1. Delgado, *Monseñor, Pro-manuscrito* (BRP). Idem, *Óscar A. Romero Biografía*, 40-41.

2. Idem, *Monseñor, Pro-manuscrito*, 43.

3. Ibid., 36.

4. Handwritten copy of Óscar Romero's reflection on his father's death. (BRP) Spanish citation: "*¡Mi papá...ha muerto! Padre mío, yo que cada tarde dirigía mis miradas al lejano oriente, enviándote cariñoso mi recuerdo lejano, te contemplaba en el corredor de mi inolvidable casa, reclinado en la baranda azul, te contemplaba dirigiendo tu miradas al ocaso donde estaba tu hijo. Recuerdo te oí una vez, 'el poniente..! ay, los que ya declinamos al poniente!' Y hoy, papá, ¿quién responde a mi mirada filial? Mi madre. ¡Ah sí, mi mamá! Pero y tu, papá querido?¡Ah! A tí ya no te contemplo vivo...*"

5. James R. Brockman, *Romero: A Life* (New York: Orbis Books, 1989), 38.

6. Ibid., 22; Maier, *Monseñor Romero: Maestro de Espiritualidad*, 28. Spanish citation: "*ser con Cristo un crucificado que redime. Con Cristo ser un resucitado que reparte resurrección y vida.*"

7. Maier, *Monseñor Romero*, 24; Brockman, *Romero: A Life*, 50.

8. Ibid., 25-26; Maier, *Monseñor Romero*, 28-29; Brockman, *Romero: A Life*.

9. Delgado, *Óscar A. Romero Biografía*, 27.

10. Ibid., 30-31.

11. *Archivo de la Provincial Centroamericana de la Compania de Jesús*, December 9, 1940 (APCSJ). Spanish citation: "*Mi querido amiguito: El Sr. Arzobispo me informa esta Vd. en deseo de ingresar al Seminario para lo cual, a pesar de sus Buenos deseos, tiene Vd. No pocas dificultades. Sabiéndolo yo me apresuro a suplicarle se venga Vd. por aquí, por este seminario de San José de la Montana, cuanto antes para que lo examinemos y veamos modo de solucionarle las dificultades...*"

12. Rodolfo Cardenal, *Historia de una Esperanza, Vida de Rutilio Grande*, 38.

13. Letter from Rutilio Grande to Alvaro Echarri, S.J., September 24, 1947 (APCSJ).

14. Letter from Archbishop Chávez y González to Rutilio Grande, June 3, 1947 (APCSJ). Spanish citation: "*Para mantener tu santa vocación, tu deber principal radica en alimentar siempre el "ideal," llegar a ser sacerdote, con la gracia de Dios y la protección de la Santísima Virgen María.*"

15. Letter from Rutilio Grande to Alvaro Echarri, S.J., August 15, 1947 (APCSJ).

Spanish citation: "*Lo he venido pensando desde hace algún tiempo y ahora he querido manifestárselo: Ya desde que estuve en el Seminario, me atrajo la Vocación Misionera; se lo que significa, Padre, y fue entonces una de las cosas que me movieron a entrar a la Compañía con la esperanza de ser un DIA Misionero entre infieles.*"

16. Letter from Fr. Echarri to Rutilio Grande, September 17, 1947 (APCSJ).

17. Cardenal, *Historia de una Esperanza*, 51-53.

18. Ibid., 54.

19. Letter from Rutilio Grande to Vice Provincial, July 8, 1951 (APCSJ). Spanish citation: "*Gracias a Dios voy de bien en mejor. Esta gordura que he conseguido a raíz de lo de Panamá, me ayuda, según lo voy experimentando, para todo.*"

20. Ibid. Spanish citation: "*…me ayuda mucho aún para la salud, como lo he notado desde que pasé de Santa Tecla al Seminario.*"

21. Ibid. Spanish citation: "*…me ayuda a mi carácter un tanto introvertido.*"

22. Ibid. Spanish citation: "*…cuidaré de alimentarme bien y de tomar la siesta ordinaria, pues la experiencia me ha enseñado que debo conservar la mayor tranquilidad y evitar por tanto, nerviosismos y extremos, aún en los mismos deberes.*"

23. Biographical details of Rutilio Grande Garcia, S.J. (APCSJ).

24. Letter from Rutilio Grande to Vice-provincial, Agustín Bariáin, S.J., December 4, 1955 (APCSJ). Spanish citation: "*me dijo que podía estar completamente tranquilo. Eso mismo decía yo en mi interior desde ya hacia tiempo.*"

25. Letter from Rutilio Grande to Flavio Grande, July 24, 1955 (APCSJ). Spanish citation: "*La levantada a las seis de la mañana…A continuación una hora de oración y la santa Misa para comenzar santamente el DIA. El desayuno a las ocho y cuarto para luego entregarse de lleno al estudio que es nuestro deber primordial a fin de formarnos unos perfectos sabios a gloria de Dios.*"

26. Letter from Rutilio Grande to Flavio Grande, July 24, 1955 (APCSJ).

27. Cardenal, *Historia de una Esperanza*, 60.

28. Interview with Rutilio Sánchez, July 1, 2014. Spanish citation: "*café con leche.*"

29. Letter from Archbishop Chávez y González to Rutilio Grande, July 18, 1959 (APCSJ). Spanish citation: "*Con un afectuoso y cariñoso saludo te envío esta carta en la víspera de tu ordenación sacerdotal; con ella van mis oraciones particulares para que Dios Nuestro Señor y la Sma. Virgen María te guarden y protegen en tu sacerdocio, pues sin la gracia de Dios y la asistencia de la Sma. Madre, poco podremos hacer en tan sublime e incomparable estado, el SACERDOCIO.*"

30. Letter from Rutilio Grande to Marcelino Zalba, February 24, 1964. (APCSJ).

31. Cardenal, *Historia de una Esperanza*, 70-71.

Detail, photograph of mural dedicated to Rutilio Grande in El Paisnal, c. 1995.

CHAPTER 3

MINISTRY EXPERIENCE

The Second World War ended on September 2, 1945 with the formal surrender of Japan, and with the Soviet Union and the United States emerging as rival superpowers. Pope Pius XII (1939-58), whose early papacy spanned the Second World War and the Nazi Holocaust, struggled against the godless specter of Communism and the worker-priest movement rooted in concern for the working class. He also angered conservatives by promoting revision of the liturgy, which later led to the reform of Catholic worship at Vatican Council II.

In El Salvador, General Maximiliano Hernández Martínez served two terms as president (1931-44); unable to constitutionally serve another term, he suspended the Constitution in order to claim a third term without an election. The Salvadoran military and various elite groups unsuccessfully protested Martínez' illegal action, but a group of students eventually organized a general strike that led to Martínez fleeing to Guatemala. For a decade afterwards, the political chaos in El Salvador reinforced the alliance between the military and landowners who were determined to maintain control of the country.

Romero and Ministry

After his return from Rome in 1944, Romero received his first pastoral assignment. For a time, he was sent as pastor to the small village of Anamorós, a locale so small that it lacked a store, running water, and light. For several months Romero's younger brother Gaspar accompanied him. Gaspar found the impoverished circumstances difficult, but Óscar embraced the assignment with: "One must not protest."[1]

Life was simple. Romero rose early around 4:00 a.m. and bathed with water drawn from the convent well. During the day, he gathered groups of children to catechize. The younger children he engaged in games; the older children were taught practical skills. Romero used his interaction with them to give guidance. He visited the smaller surrounding towns of Polorós, Nueva Esparta, and Concepción de Oriente. Although involved in his ministry in Anamorós, a few months after his arrival Romero was assigned to San Miguel. At the news of his transfer, the people of Anamorós wept, as even with the brief time of his pastoral presence, they had become fond of him.[2]

The bishop of San Miguel, Miguel Ángel Machado y Escobar, assigned Romero as secretary of the diocese where he would dedicate twenty-three years of his life. Over time, Romero acquired additional responsibilities. He was pastor not only of the cathedral parish of San Miguel, but also the smaller parishes of Santo Domingo and San Francisco.[3] The image of Our Lady of Peace, patroness of El Salvador, had been temporarily placed inside the church of San Francisco while work on the cathedral was being completed. Motivated by his lifelong devotion to the Blessed Mother, Romero assumed care of the holy image, and during his years in San Miguel, undertook the task of building its cathedral to further cultivate the devotion to Our Lady of Peace among the faithful. The deepening of local popular devotion to her became a unifying element of his efforts.[4]

In San Miguel, Romero's daily schedule included rising early to pray until 5:00 a.m., and then celebrating Mass. After breakfast, Romero tried to leave time to play the organ before heading to the archdiocesan office to work. Often in the afternoon, he visited the sick and the elderly.[5] To nourish his own spiritual life, he established a personal hour of devotion each evening in front of the Blessed Sacrament which included the recitation of the rosary and meditation.

The years in San Miguel were busy ones. As Brockman outlines in his work, Romero was a relentless worker in the diocese. Aside from his primary responsibility as secretary to the archbishop and serving as pastor to several parishes, Romero founded a group of Alcoholics Anonymous. He went to the city jails to visit inmates. He was involved in religious education and preparation for First Communion. He went to the countryside to attend to the pastoral needs of the more geographically isolated. He also promoted and supported several apostolic groups among them the *Cursillos de Cristiandad*, Caritas, and the Holy Rosary Association.[6] He organized groups of workers who shined shoes or delivered newspapers or similar services, teaching them how to be good workers.[7] Furthermore during these years, Romero became well known for his preaching, which was broadcasted throughout the city on Sunday.

His twenty-three years of generous pastoral ministry to the people of San Miguel ended in 1967 with the retirement of Bishop Machado. The new bishop, Lorenzo Michele Joseph Graziano, named Romero secretary-general of the national bishops' conference. Romero went to reside in the seminary in San Salvador ready to pursue his new responsibilities with his customary enthusiasm and efficiency.

Arriving at the seminary, however, Romero's reputation had preceded him. During his years in San Miguel, his stern appraisal of brother priests had done little to engender affection. Romero had always rigorously tried to integrate a high and demanding sense of priesthood into every aspect of his priestly life. Unfortunately, this attitude had engendered an intolerance with regard to the human weaknesses of his brother priests. Furthermore, Romero's shy and introverted personality made it difficult for him to socially engage others. Consequently, he was not warmly welcomed to the seminary of San José de La Montaña in San Salvador.

During these years he first became acquainted with the Jesuit Father Rutilio Grande. Two years before Romero arrived, Rutilio had been assigned to the seminary as prefect of discipline, professor of pastoral theology, and director of pastoral ministry. At that time Rutilio Grande was one of the few Salvadoran Jesuits living at the seminary. Perhaps, as some have suggested, Grande empathized with Romero's plight of the unwelcome outsider. In any event, by some accounts Rutilio eased the tensions between his own Jesuit brothers and Romero.

On April 21, 1970, the nuncio notified Romero that he had been chosen to serve as auxiliary bishop of San Salvador. Prior to accepting, Romero consulted with two of his spiritual directors, one a Jesuit and the other a member of Opus Dei.[8] Romero, inclined to scrupulosity, was in conflict over whether to accept. On June 8, Romero began a retreat to prepare for his episcopal ordination; even two years after his episcopal consecration, Romero would still struggle with the same doubts that he had indicated in the spiritual notes from his retreat. His scrupulosity and his desire for perfection tormented him throughout his life.

Romero's spiritual notes from that retreat are very revealing. He speaks of "the sweetness and the intimacy with Jesus,"[9] and he dedicates his episcopacy to the Sacred Heart of Jesus as his patron.[10] He wishes to offer reparation to the wounded Heart suffering from the affliction of humanity's sin.[11] His notes express the deep ecstasy that enraptured his soul.

In addressing the practicalities of the ceremony and celebration of his Episcopal ordination, Romero asked Rutilio Grande to assume responsibility for the occasion. Once Grande accepted, the Jesuit invested his considerable liturgical and organizational talents into the preparations. In a letter to his Provincial Francisco Estrada, Grande shared: "I have been pressed from many directions which began when I started the preparatory work for Monseñor Romero's [Episcopal] Consecration."[12]

Romero never forgot Rutilio's contribution to one of the most significant days of his life. In a letter to Grande on June 22, 1972, Romero recalled his profound gratitude: "...on this same day I had a reunion in the Basilica where the altar of that unforgettable concelebration took place...and I have remembered with renewed sentiments of gratitude and affection all the kindnesses, activities and sacrifices that you assumed along with the good lay friends to bring about that unforgettable liturgy in which you were its heart and soul."[13]

Romero's episcopal ordination took place on June 21, 1970, and although it is a date associated with honoring Our Lady of Peace, his ascension to the episcopacy was not a unifying event. The church community of San Salvador at that time was stirred by the twin tides of abject poverty and suffering, and challenged by the insights and direction of an emerging liberation theology. Considering himself a dutiful son of the Church, Romero faithfully followed any directive of Rome and the Holy See. But in regard to the documents of Medellín, the new auxiliary bishop did not share the same commitment as did San Salvador's bishops, Archbishop Chávez y González and Auxiliary Bishop Arturo Rivera y Damas.

Romero accepted the legitimacy of the documents of the Second Vatican Council, and he felt that they were sufficient in themselves.[14] Although he considered the documents of Medellín to be interpretations and adaptations of Vatican II, he nevertheless questioned their fidelity to the doctrines of the Fathers of the Church.[15] In spite of Romero's spiritual embrace of his appointment to the episcopacy, his practical attitudes and values were rooted in his background as one of the "*Romani*." His Roman orientation was a source of significant conflict for a number of priests who saw the conservative Romero at odds with the directions articulated by the Latin American Bishops gathered in Medellín, Colombia, in 1968. Furthermore, for the clergy who were struggling to find a pastoral approach to serve the poor, the expense of Romero's Episcopal ordination was considered scandalous in a poverty-riddled country.

The day following Romero's Episcopal ordination, about two hundred clergy, religious, and laity gathered to inaugurate a national pastoral week to study ways in which the Church of El Salvador might implement the teachings of Vatican II and Medellín. The week's conclusions promoted the training and formation of the laity so that they would be prepared to take an active role in both the life of the Church and evangelization. Lay leaders, catechists, and delegates of the Word were envisioned as active participants in the ministry of the Church alongside priests and religious.[16] Romero participated in the week of study and initially accepted its conclusions. Later, however, he withdrew his support. Even during the following four years as auxiliary bishop of San Salvador, he rarely attended meetings of the clergy. He felt the meetings merely provided a forum for the priests to complain about the Church and the Pope.[17] As regards to pastoral matters, Romero was predisposed to the advice of Archbishop Emanuele Gerada, the papal nuncio and one of his strong supporters.[18] Painfully aware of Romero's Roman favoritism, the priests distrusted the new auxiliary.

In 1971, the editor of the diocesan newspaper *Orientación* was removed for being too progressive and liberal, and Romero, as auxiliary bishop, was named in his place. Romero's new editorial direction was markedly conservative. He used his newly found "pulpit" to openly criticize anything that gave the appearance of fomenting anti-Roman discontent or of supporting Marxist ideologies and communism. In the issue of *Orientación* dated May 27, 1973, he publicly accused the Jesuits of implementing a priestly formation program based on Marxist principles. In response, Archbishop Chávez y González formed a committee to investigate Romero's accusation against the Jesuits. Although the investigation found the accusation to be unsubstantiated, Romero maintained his negative assessment of the Jesuits. Under his editorial leadership, the diocesan newspaper maintained a decisively "Roman" position. The conservative nature of *Orientación* led to a progressive decline in subscription, but Romero refused to change. The newspaper soon sank into debt and lost its readership.

In December 1974, Romero was ordained Bishop of Santiago de María. He interpreted his selection as bishop as a public affirmation by Rome of his pastoral style and service. Yet in Santiago de María, Romero would come into direct pastoral contact with the reality of the poor. Ironically, it would become his transforming experience. In his own words: "There I indeed ran head-on into [abject] misery. With those children that would die merely because of the water that they drank, with those peasants ill-treated in the coffee fields…"[19]

Romero was the second bishop of Santiago de María, which had a population of about half a million. An oppressively poor area, most of the diocese's twenty parishes were without a priest, and the priests who were available attended to more than one parish.[20] Socioeconomically, the land was in the hands of about 30% of the population while the other 70% were campesinos who worked primarily in the coffee plantations owned by the wealthy landowners. As schools were scarce, over 40% of the people were illiterate. Most housing was made of reed and mud.[21]

As he had done in San Miguel, in his new diocese Romero directed his pastoral energies toward promoting the sacramental life of the people and to preaching. For the first time in many years, however, probably since the days of his own boyhood, Romero came into direct contact with the humble people of El Salvador. As he ventured out to be with the people, he discovered them living in deplorable poverty. He mounted speakers on a jeep and he traveled to the countryside. With music and songs, he gathered the people, and used those opportunities to evangelize them and celebrate baptisms and marriages.[22] Men worked excessive hours in the coffee fields but received miserly pay from the landowners. Those landowners, however, had been Romero's friends; he wanted to believe that they were good Christians who treated their workers justly. To his sorrow and disappointment he gradually discovered that this was not the case.

Disillusioned by the innate selfishness of the monied class and overwhelmed by the insidious poverty of the poor people of his diocese, Romero began to search for new understandings. At his first meeting with his clergy in Santiago de María, Romero expressed his deepest desire: "Help me to see clearly."[23] For the clergy, these words were a sign of hope. They had feared that Romero would follow the style of their previous bishop who had been closed to the spirit of Vatican II and Medellín. For Romero, the reality of the poor with whom he was in close contact began to reveal truths that would lead him implacably along the road of transformation that he so desired, to a culmination that he could not then have imagined.

The brief two years (1974-76) that Romero was bishop of Santiago de María were a period of intense insight and change. Diez and Macho, authors of a rich account of Romero's time there, identified four critical events that led Romero to re-evaluate his earlier ideals regarding the government's relationship with the people of El Salvador.[24]

First, on June 21, 1975, forty soldiers of the National Guard of El Salvador attacked the small hamlet of Tres Calles abusing its inhabitants and killing four men without cause or provocation. When news of the attack was reported, his clergy encouraged Romero to register a public protest to the government. Convinced that the matter could be handled in writing, Romero sent a letter to his brother bishops informing them of the attack and asking for their advice and support. He also wrote a lengthy letter to The Republic's President Arturo Armando Molina detailing the events and requesting that the matter be handled justly and promptly. To his surprise and disappointment, nothing was done.

Two months later, on August 16, 1975, another jolting eye-opener occurred. Father Juan Machado Merino, a Passionist priest from Spain who was returning to his parish in Santiago de María, was detained at the airport in San Salvador, refused permission to re-enter the country and without explanation or reason was returned directly to Spain. Again Romero wrote a letter to the President of the Republic questioning the treatment of the priest and demanding that Father Merino be allowed to return to El Salvador. Although Romero met the following day with the President, who apologized for the mistake and assured him that Father Merino could return, the priest's return was delayed for months. Despite these troubling events, Romero maintained a temporizing position regarding the degree of danger facing the poor and the church ministers at that time. Romero believed that his personal relationship with the President and other government officials and influential people would help him to manage the situation.

For the committed religious community of his diocese, however, tensions and difficulties began to escalate. With the unwarranted expulsion of Father Merino, the Passionist community in El Salvador feared for their safety.[25] The Passionists had established the Centro de Naranjos for the formation of lay leaders in light of the directives of Vatican II. Acting out of caution, Romero closed the Center citing the need for proper evaluation of its activities and goals. In response, the Passionist community presented a detailed report on the mission and goals of the Centro. After numerous exchanges with Romero, the Provincial of the Passionist Community requested that a final decision be made regarding the future of the Centro and its work.

Finally, according to first-hand accounts, Romero agonized over the matter of the Centro. As was his custom, he invested considerable time in prayer. He also sought advice from a neighboring priest, a new strategy that was becoming part of his style of decision-making. Finally, on December 13, 1975, Romero wrote an extensive letter to the Passionist Provincial. "I beseech, then, my esteemed Father Vicar, that taking in faith my sincere expression of appreciation in favor of the priestly service of the Passionist Community in Jiquilisco, that all lack of confidence or misunderstanding be dispelled that could be an obstacle to such a valuable collaboration..."[26] Romero continued dialogue to address any remaining fears and doubts about the Centro. He embraced the exchange and visited the Centro several times to immerse himself in the reality of the people's formation. Through his involvement with the Centro, Romero gained a deeper under-standing of the reality endured by the humble people of El Salvador. He began to realize that the process of consciousness-raising was helping the suffering and oppressed people to be able to respond to the injustices in their lives. Romero was beginning to realize, too, the poignancy and validity of the documents of Medellín, and, indeed, that they were authentically following the directives of Vatican II.

This series of powerful experiences impacted Romero's personal level of social consciousness. The massacre of the innocent in Tres Calles, the unjust expulsion of Juan Macho Merino, the threats against the members of the Passionist community, and the pastoral formation and activities of the Centro Los Naranjos, gave him a powerfully new perception of the dangerous experiences lived by the poor and their committed Christian ministers. In Santiago de María, Romero came face to face with the dire poverty of his homeland. His years in Rome and the subsequent years in administrative ministry in El Salvador had insulated him from the reality into which he had been born. But now, re-acclimated, he responded immediately and concretely.

He opened up the Cathedral Church at night for the men who worked in the coffee plantation but had no place to sleep. He directed that the workers should always be served something warm to drink. At night, he spent time visiting with the men, conversing with them and hearing about the difficulties of their daily lives and struggles. These experiences moved him to exclaim: "This is not work [for me]. The greatest gift is to be here."[27] At this significant juncture in his life, the testimony of the poor themselves dramatically propelled Romero along the road of radical transformation.

His lifelong love for the Eucharist became embodied in the suffering of the poor. In Romero's two years as bishop of Santiago de María, he learned to identify with and truly love the "crucified peoples" of his homeland. In the faces of the poor and in their stories of sickening oppression and injustice, Romero's devotion to the Crucified Jesus and the Eucharist took on a human identity.

In February of 1977 Bishop Gerada, the papal nuncio, announced the selection of his recommended candidate Óscar Romero as Arch-bishop of San Salvador. The nuncio's choice had been based on consultation with some of the more powerful political and economic figures in the country, who approved of the candidacy of the bishop whom they considered part of their social class. The nuncio also enlisted the support of some of the superiors of religious communities in El Salvador.[28]

The news disappointed many of the clergy. In their previous experience of Romero, they had found him to be reluctant to embrace the "new" pastoral activities and methods. They were aware of Romero's earlier public letters and articles that had criticized the Jesuit pastoral work in Aguilares, and which questioned the "political theology" that the Jesuits were promoting at the Universidad Centroamericana (UCA). His articles had directly named the priests he criticized. For the clergy and the faithful who were hoping for a new direction for the church of El Salvador, Romero was not an encouraging choice.

Despite the fact that Romero had criticized not only the Society of Jesus, but also the Jesuit pastoral work at Aguilares, once again, Rutilio Grande stepped forward to support Romero by encouraging his Jesuit confreres in Aguilares: "We must help the new archbishop, even though he is not the one we most like. We cannot leave him alone in these moments."[29]

Shortly after the nuncio's announcement of his appointment to the archbishopric, Romero addressed a small gathering of priests where it was clear from their polite but restrained reception that his appointment was a disappointment.[30] Nevertheless, his episcopal ordination was celebrated on February 22, 1977. Romero would be Archbishop of San Salvador for a brief period of three years. He could not have predicted what was to be required of him during those years.

Rutilio Grande

Unlike Romero with his several decades of immersion in academic studies and administration, Rutilio Grande had never been totally removed from pastoral ministry. From 1951-53 as sub-prefect of discipline and teacher of Latin, Spanish, geography, and history in the seminary of San José de la Montaña in San Salvador, and again in 1960-62, he worked in the formation and education of those young men. Even during his years of study in Oña, Spain, he found opportunities to interact with the people of the town. He had a special gift of working with groups of young people of ages 12-16,[31] organizing catechetical programs as a way of not only teaching the faith, but also involving the townspeople in the ministry. In each of these ministerial situations, Rutilio demonstrated a talent for working effectively with groups, enabling them to engage in their own learning. In 1965, when he returned to the seminary of San José de la Montaña, Father Grande began to exhibit his creativity regarding seminary formation.

Grande's study (1963-64) in Belgium at Lumen Vitae, a renowned catechetical and pastoral institute inspired his approach to his assignment in the seminary. The spirit generated by the Second Vatican Council positioned Lumen Vitae as a meeting place for international exchange among pastoralists from Africa, Asia, Latin America, and North America. While at Lumen Vitae, Rutilio was immersed in the latest catechetical methods of the time and was exposed to the leading experts in the field. He took his exams in the areas of Bible, liturgy, doctrine, psychology and sociology of religion, method and history of catechesis, and introduction to pastoral theology, receiving his diploma in Pastoral Catechesis with Great Distinction. He returned to El Salvador invigorated by the new insights that he had acquired in Brussels.

Returning to the seminary, Rutilio drew upon his pride in being Salvadoran, often referring to himself as like *"café con leche"* (coffee with milk). He was friendly, respectful and attentive to the seminarians, concerned for their welfare and for the best preparation for their priesthood.

In a short time, Grande began to find ways to open seminary formation to the reality of the outside world. As the seminary professor of pastoral theology, he wanted the seminarians to not only engage directly with the realities of the people of El Salvador, but also to be actively involved in the learning processes. During the summer months he organized the seminarians for trips (*Campo-Misión*) to the surrounding towns. The young men visited families in their homes, encouraged to look at the reality that each family was living (*to See*). Each group had a leader chosen from among their peers. The main objective was to come to know the families. Once they were able to draw a profile of each household, they evaluated the situation in the light of the Word of God (*to Judge*). From this information, Grande helped them to design a parish mission, based on real needs, to be given in each parish (*to Act*). It was not uncommon for eighty seminarians to accompany Rutilio to a town for these pastoral visits. An article in the Archdiocesan newspaper noted the seminarians' mission activity and concluded that this "great experience without a doubt will help the seminarians discover future dimensions of the priesthood and the needs of our people."[32] Making pastoral theology real prepared the future priests of El Salvador to actualize a new understanding of Church as articulated in the teachings of the Second Vatican Council and Medellín.

Grande's formation objective was to involve the seminarians in the concrete realities of the lives of the people that they would one day serve as priests. Gatherings dedicated to the outcomes of the Second Vatican Council were held at the seminary, and despite some resistance on the part of some of the clergy, the seminarians were included. They also participated in a week at the seminary dedicated to Pastoral Ministry initiated by Archbishop Chávez y González.[33] Father Grande enabled the young men to take evening courses in theology outside of the seminary at the UCA. When a religious sister brought her nursing skills to the seminary infirmary, this simple decision brought a feminine presence to the male dominated world of San José de la Montaña.[34] Rutilio could be seen visiting those who were ill, bringing them comfort. During his tenure, Rutilio also gave attention to the athletic activities of the seminarians.[35] In a letter that he wrote to a friend, Rutilio reported with great pride that the school had won a major game. Grande's students benefited greatly from his studies at Lumen Vitae.

Aside from his teaching responsibility as professor of pastoral theology, Grande taught courses in Sacred Scripture. Father Octavio Cruz later recalled how Grande made the Scriptural texts come alive, masterfully relating Scripture to the human condition of the times. Father Grande showed the text speaking to current history, and made his students attentive to God being present in the world. He awoke in Cruz a hunger for God, which helped solidify his priestly vocation.[36]

Grande's innovative approach to formation was applauded by some and frowned upon by those who promoted the more traditional seminary formation. The tension between these two positions intensified over the next five years. Yet the seminarians themselves embraced the new approaches, as Rutilio had the ability to recognize the talent and skill of each of them and gave them the opportunity to use it.

Decades later, as they recalled their seminary years under the leadership of Rutilio Grande, some of his former students spoke of how they perceived that Grande had placed great confidence in them by handing over the planning process for some of these endeavors to them.[37] Others remembered with fondness the genuine care and affection that Rutilio had expressed toward the seminarians.[38] Rutilio took the young men to popular celebrations in the surrounding towns and made sure that the seminarians enjoyed the cultural expressions of their homeland. He was present to the seminarians as they mourned the death of family members.[39] On one occasion, when he comforted a seminarian whose brother was dealing with depression, Rutilio drew from his own experience with bouts of depression to give the young man advice.[40]

Rutilio made himself available to support the seminarians in their deliberations or decisions. On more than one occasion, he defended them against the unjustified criticism from the clergy. In one particular instance, the seminarians were not in agreement with the political stance of the President of El Salvador and refused to sing at the annual celebration of the Patronal Feast of *El Salvador del Mundo*— The Savior of the World—in the Cathedral. Although distressed by their decision, Rutilio respected it, and it fell to him to inform Archbishop Chávez y González that the seminarians would not be singing at the event.[41] On another occasion, a small group of seminarians, unhappy with seminary life in San Salvador, were planning to transfer to Mexico to continue their priestly formation. Finding out about the intended "coup," Grande spoke with each of the students. Listening carefully to their reasons, he facilitated a meeting for them with Archbishop Chávez y González where they could share their concerns.[42] On yet another occasion, the seminarians protested the quality of food that was being served at the seminary.[43] And again, as in each such situation, Father Grande supported the seminarians as they expressed their opinions and concerns.

In spite of challenges, Grande not only loved seminary formation, but he excelled at it. Nevertheless, tensions were escalating over the type of seminary formation that Rutilio was implementing. Two events led to Grande's resignation from the seminary.

At the National Pastoral Ministry Week, held a few days after Romero had been named Auxiliary Bishop of San Salvador, an editorial committee had been formed. After working with the conclusions from the week, the committee submitted their work to be reviewed by the bishops. Unexpectedly, the conclusions were changed by those few bishops who had attended. The new version excluded any mention of either the Second Vatican Council or Medellín. Although Rutilio had not been in charge of the event, he had been elected to work on the final editing. Respectfully, yet strongly, he spoke in defense of honoring the original work of the editing committee, a stance that was not well accepted by some of the bishops.

The following month in the Cathedral, Father Rutilio delivered the sermon for the annual Patronal Feast of El Salvador del Mundo. Grande, conscientiously preparing the sermon yet setting aside the traditional cultural approach to the celebration, focused on the serious responsibility of the government and the church to transform the country's unjust situations and structures. The bishops in attendance criticized Grande's presentation of Jesus as the primary revolutionary in history who had transformed the direction of salvation history.[44] Nor were the bishops pleased with Grande's frequent references to the Constitutional rights promised all Salvadorans. Nevertheless, at the end of the Mass, the President of El Salvador, Fidel Sánchez Hernández, congratulated Grande on his fine sermon and asked for a copy, later giving Rutilio a copy of the Constitution of El Salvador. While praised by President Sánchez, Grande later found himself sternly chastised by one of the bishops. In a letter to a Jesuit friend, he expressed his dismay and confusion at the bishop's treatment of him.

By November 30, 1969, Grande felt that he could no longer effectively carry out his seminary responsibilities. He wrote a detailed letter to the Jesuit Provincial explaining his reasons for resigning from the seminary, reminding the Provincial that he had earlier expressed his desire to leave his position. He emphasized that his decision was based neither on impulse nor stemming from depression, desolation, or discouragement.[45] After his experience at Lumen Vitae, Grande had embraced his assignment to San José de la Montaña in 1965 with great enthusiasm. But now, having lost the trust of the bishops and others, he felt in good conscience that he could no longer remain at the seminary. He also wrote a similarly detailed letter to Archbishop Chávez y González informing him of his decision to resign. True to himself, in both of these letters, Grande had not only meticulously explained his rationale for his decision but that he had grounded his decision in God through prayer.

With great sadness, in 1970, Grande resigned from his responsibilities at the Seminary of San José de la Montaña. His love for God, the Church, and the Society of Jesus had led him to fully dedicate himself to the formation of future priests. As one of his former students said: "If anyone in El Salvador is responsible for the creation of a new understanding of Church, it would be Rutilio Grande. He prepared a whole generation of seminarians for the priesthood, and it was from among them that the martyrs of El Salvador were chosen. We owe him a debt of gratitude."[46]

And, in fact, many of the priests who were killed during the years of the Civil War in El Salvador had either been taught by Father Grande in the seminary, or were known by him. Among the martyrs of El Salvador were Octaviano Ortiz, Ernesto Barrera, Alirio Macías, Rafael Palacios, and Alfonso Navarro, who had all been in formation under the direction of Rutilio Grande in the seminary of San José de La Montaña.[47]

Following his time in San José de la Montaña, Grande became prefect of discipline at Externado San José, the Jesuit high school for boys in San Salvador. A Jesuit brother recalled Grande's successful service there. He was not only committed to the ministry, but also loved by his students. In handling difficult situations with either the students or faculty, he took care that his decisions were balanced and fair.[48] The ministry of working in a high school with young Salvadorans, however, was temporary and lasted only a year.

At the end of the academic year of 1972, Rutilio was sent for additional study at the Latin American Pastoral Institute (IPLA) in Quito, Ecuador. As he wrote to his Jesuit friend Jaime Vera Fajardo, his time in Quito was particularly rich and satisfying: "I am extremely happy with my course. It is well worth it. It is a Lumen Vitae on American soil, with roots in the problem of Latin America; it is timely and profound, with good teachers."[49] The eight-month course put Grande in contact with internationally known theologians and pastoralists. Concurrently, Grande himself was coming to the attention of many outside of El Salvador. In a very short time, he impressed his fellow IPLA students and teachers with the methods that he used in seminary formation, and with his projected plans for "rural ministry" (*pastoral campesino*).

In years to come, many of those he met at IPLA not only maintained correspondence with him but kept track of his work. Alfonso López Trujillo, Secretary General of CELAM (Episcopal Conference of Latin America) wrote: "I follow with much joy your work and what you are doing to awaken enthusiasm. I will be going, God willing, around February 10, to the Episcopal Assembly. Hopefully, I will have the pleasure of seeing you."[50] Segundo Galilea, a professor of liberation theology in the IPLA program responded to a letter from Rutilio, expressing his pleasure at hearing that his former student continued his commitment in rural ministry.[51] Rodrigo, another IPLA classmate writes to Rutilio from Mexico letting him know of a recent meeting where he met Sister María de Jesús Ibarra from the agricultural region of Yakima, Washington: "She came with a Chicano priest and it was the best part of the meeting. They have been able to conscientize their bishops and priests and to commit many to work in favor of the oppressed Chicanos (which are the majority). They now form a powerful lobbying force within the American church and society."[52] In later years, pastoral leaders in El Salvador and beyond sought out Grande for his expertise in rural ministry.

On July 28, 1972 Rutilio successfully completed the Pastoral Course at IPLA. His studies included the History and Sociology of Latin America, Anthropology, Ecclesiology, World and Pastoral Theology, Sacred Scripture, Evangelization, Catechesis and Liturgy, Base Christian Communities, and Collaborative Pastoral Ministry (*Pastoral de conjunto*). He returned to El Salvador with an enriched understanding of ministry.

Earlier that year, the Jesuit Provincial Miguel Francisco Estrada had written to ask Rutilio to consider engaging in a new ministry. In his letter of March 10, 1972, Estrada wrote: "I would like it, Rutilio, if you could begin thinking about our ministries. It isn't easy, but those who are interested have asked for it and I believe that we can count on the collaboration of other Jesuits and non-Jesuits. Experts in pastoral work, liturgy, sacraments etc… So that, we can begin thinking about a team who can later…help us update our apostolic activities."[53]

The new pastoral opportunities that Father Estrada was suggesting attracted Rutilio. Interacting in IPLA with men and women from all over Latin America and beyond, his horizons broadened. In order to visit other pastoral sites in Panama, Riobamba (in Ecuador), and Honduras, he asked his Jesuit Provincial to extend his time beyond completion of the IPLA program. He received approval from Father Estrada to do so.[54] For some time, the Society of Jesus had been discerning how to live a truly authentic response to their founding spirit. In reviewing their history in Central America, and in light of the new challenges presented by the Second Vatican Council and Medellín, the Jesuits concluded that new apostolic works with new directions were necessary: ministries that would address the realities of Church and society, and would confront the abuse of power.

Carefully and prayerfully, Grande reflected upon the new pastoral movements that were stirring within the Church and the Company of Jesus. From his early years in Jesuit formation, Rutilio demonstrated a fundamental desire to seek the will of God. He had once written to the Jesuit Provincial: "I have entrusted the matter to God and I have given it thought; but I do not confide in myself. In all sincerity and in all openness, I place myself in your hands so that you can decide what is best… I will go to the place that obedience indicates…"[55] Now, however, Rutilio was also attentive to the signs of the times and the needs of the people of his time and place.

Prayerful reflections led Grande to formulate what he called "My Primary and Fundamental Pastoral Option" (*Mi Opción Pastoral Primaria y Fundamental*). This consisted of three fundamental commitments: that ministry be a collaborative team effort; that pastoral work be carried out in a rural area among "*campesinos*" (peasant workers); that the goal of the ministry be comprehensive and integral development rooted in a Christian foundation. He returned to El Salvador in the middle of 1972 with the intention of finding a way to implement his fundamental pastoral option.

In mid-September of that year, he met with Jesuit Salvador Carranza to discuss this new pastoral initiative. In Santa Tecla, El Salvador, they made a retreat where they refined and redesigned the envisioned rural pastoral plan: to evangelize in order to recreate a church of living communities with renewed men and women who, as pastoral agents would direct their own human destiny. They decided to add two more Jesuits to the fledging team and chose the parish of Our Lord of Mercies in the town of Aguilares, which combined an urban and rural setting, as the site for the new pastoral endeavor. Known primarily for its sugar cane production and processing on large estates, the area included three large sugar cane mills. Playing an essential role in the economics of the area, the sugar cane industry also carried weighty political implications.

Initially, Rutilio preferred to select another location, as the parish boundaries of Aguilares extended to his hometown of El Paisnal. He would rather have had more pastoral objectivity. In the end, the fact that his beloved mentor Archbishop Chávez y González wanted Aguilares as the site persuaded Rutilio to accede to Aguilares as the site.[56]

In August, Archbishop Chávez y González wrote to Rutilio to share the outcomes of a pastoral gathering that he had attended in Guatemala. In acknowledging Rutilio's plan to become involved in rural ministry he wrote: "In Esquipulas it was said, that a priest dedicated to the formation of peasant workers (*campesinos*) …is as important as those who work in parishes."[57]

A month later on September 24, 1972, the Archbishop formally assigned Padre Grande as pastor of the parish of Our Lord of Mercies in the city of Aguilares. As in the past, the archbishop totally trusted that Rutilio was the right person for the parish. Grande also proceeded with the respect and confidence of the Society of Jesus.

After some initial discussion, the team of four Jesuits, Rutilio Grande, Benigno Fernández, Jesús A. Bengoechea, and Salvador Carranza divided the parish into two zones. They organized the city into ten sectors and the area of the countryside into fifteen sectors. Going out in pairs, much like in the Gospel story, each pastoral team of priests and lay collaborators spent a day visiting the families of a division. After each visit, they synthesized the information they had gathered to design follow-up "missions." A Carmelite sister who accompanied Rutilio Grande to the countryside recounted one such visit:

> Rutilio Grande and the Sister had walked for the better part of the morning to reach the home of an older couple who lived at quite a distance. It was noon by the time they arrived. Doña Barbarita welcomed her unexpected guests delightedly, but then as she realized that it was lunch time and she had nothing to offer them, she became embarrassed. She only had tortillas to share with them. Rutilio put her at ease, assuring her that tortillas were good. Doña Barbarita then offered to prepare an egg that she had. Rutilio asked her to hard-boil it, and asked if they had beans, which of course they did. When she brought him the hard-boiled egg, he took it and divided it into four equal parts giving each person a portion. As they ate the food, Doña Barbarita was beside herself with joy exclaiming that she felt that God was present. And Rutilio reminded her that in the Kingdom of God, they would all share in the banquet.[58]

Rutilio left exclaiming: "Women such as this one can transmit so much about God and they are the ones who have communicated it to us. That woman has great faith and her faith will help us all."[59]

In fact, Rutilio's prophetic assessment of the woman would come true. Years later as the violence of the war intensified, countless people were murdered and their bodies left in the streets. Despite the danger, Doña Barbarita organized a group of women who went into the streets gathering the discarded dead bodies, bathing them and preparing them for burial.

By their innovative approach to rural evangelization, visiting each household in both the urban and rural sectors of Aguilares, Rutilio and his Jesuit brothers prepared many lay and religious leaders. After carrying out the initial one-day visit, the information they gathered would be codified and used to create a fifteen-day-long mission in each of the sites. During the mission, the priests from the team lived with different families, eating and sleeping in their homes. Unfortunately, at this juncture Rutilio discovered that he was suffering from severe diabetes and his medical condition made it impossible for him to fully participate in the process. To his disappointment, he had to limit himself to the "missions" in the urban setting of Aguilares in order to closely monitor what he ate and make any adjustments to his daily regime.

The missions that were prepared for each sector focused on the study of basic Scriptural themes with age appropriate sessions for the children and the adults. The goal of the sessions was to provide the people with basic scriptural knowledge to help them continue the celebration of God's Word on their own. During the mission, marriages and baptisms were celebrated, and the participants identified their future leaders. Later, the groups selected delegates to serve as a link between the community and the parish. The delegates were given additional formation, and a growing number of men and women assumed different ministerial roles in the growing Christian communities. After the two week mission, a priest who was assigned to the community, along with lay collaborators, accompanied the evangelization process in the groups. The ultimate goal of these efforts was the announcement of the Gospel and the formation of committed Christians.

This method of evangelizing bore much fruit. The campesinos discovered the liberating spirit of the Word of God, and they learned to incorporate it into their lives. As Salvador Carranza, S.J. observed first-hand, the campesinos gained confidence, gradually discarding the sense of inferiority which had been nurtured in them over the years. As their confidence increased, so did their ability to understand that God did not want men and women to be poor. Recognizing the injustices of their work conditions they began to organize themselves to obtain just wages and better working conditions. As one of the campesinos who participated in the process of evangelization in Aguilares recalled: "Father Rutilio never advocated the creation or organization of political groups, but it was to be expected. He would always say, 'I don't belong to one political party or another. What I am doing is preaching the gospel.' But, as we gained greater consciousness of our human rights, we began to look for ways to secure them. It seemed inevitable that we would become politically involved."[60] In time, the formation of political organizations protesting injustices toward the campesinos placed Rutilio and the Aguilares parish team in conflict with the Aguilares sugarcane landowners.

Rutilio Grande and his team members had begun their innovative approach to evangelization in 1972. Three years later in 1975, the Jesuits asked for a formal agreement between the Archdiocese of San Salvador and the Society of Jesus. At that juncture, the team would be joined by Octavio Cruz, a diocesan priest who had been taught by Grande. The two-year contract was signed with the objective that the administration of the parish in Aguilares would be eventually transferred to the diocesan clergy in San Salvador. Before that could happen, however, on March 12, 1977, the work of the Aguilares team would be tragically disrupted with the murder of Rutilio Grande and his two traveling companions.

In their lives of ministry, both Óscar Romero and Rutilio Grande generously and selflessly used their talents and abilities to serve the people of God. Although each man exercised his priestly ministry very differently, for both, their greatest desire was to be responsive to God's call in their lives and to bring the Gospel of Love and Justice to the poor and oppressed of El Salvador.

Preceding the Second Vatican Council and its imperative that the Church be in more direct connection with the modern world and its realities, Romero's call to ministry emerged during a more conservative time in the life of the Church, and his involvements followed a more traditional line. Nevertheless, born in a poor town, Romero himself was no stranger to poverty and struggle, but his years of study in the seminary and in Rome physically separated him from the harsh reality of his native land. He was immersed in a world of books so different from the humble working context he had known as a child. Even returning to his homeland, his reinsertion into his humble roots was a journey yet to be made. But by 1977 during Romero's visit to Rome, Father César Jerez, the Jesuit Provincial, commented on the remarkable shift he found in Romero. Romero's response outlined an understanding of his own personal and cultural change: "One has roots…I was born in a very poor family. I have suffered hunger, and I know what it means to work as a child…When I went to the seminary and I dedicated myself to my studies and later they send me here to Rome, I spend years and years lost in books and I start to forget my origins. I start to fashion another world for myself. Afterwards, I return to El Salvador and they give me the responsibility of being the secretary to the bishop of San Miguel. Twenty-three years of being the pastor there also submerged me among papers. And when they bring me to San Salvador as auxiliary bishop, I fall into the hands of Opus Dei. And there I remain…"[61]

Romero's episcopal ordination in 1977 as the Archbishop of El Salvador brought him a new opportunity to come into contact with the suffering poor of El Salvador. By his own admission, he had returned to the reality of his childhood roots because of his involvement with the oppressed coffee workers in Santiago de María. He acknowledged the change that others were seeing in him. He understood it not as a dramatic departure from who he had been, but rather, as a homecoming to the reality of the poor.[62]

Rutilio Grande, also born in one of the poorest little villages of El Salvador, suffered from poverty and the disintegration of family life. His Jesuit formation and studies, however, offered him the opportunity to travel to many places in South America and Europe. His travels enriched his educational and ministerial understanding. In spite of broadened experience, however, Rutilio never forgot his roots or his hometown. He maintained contact with his family through copious correspondence with his older brother Flavio, and through him with the people of his hometown of El Paisnal. He sometimes asked Flavio to deliver a message to a specific person or group in El Paisnal.

Even from a distance he was attentive to the spiritual needs of his hometown. Over the many years of Jesuit formation and study, he continuously requested pastoral attentions for El Paisnal. From Panama in 1972 he wrote Flavio: "I am happy to hear the good news of El Paisnal. Everything is due to a letter that I personally delivered to the Archbishop, when I went to say good-bye to him. In that letter I shared in rather dire terms the situation of the town and its need for a good priest or a community of sisters. I communicated to him how it was going to be left abandoned in my absence. God willing everything will be settled."[63]

Although at times Rutilio reflected on his long and intense immersion in the culture of Spain—given his years of study there and his formation in the Spanish-driven culture of his Jesuit community—in his heart he was always "*Salvadoreño*." But he also maintained correspondence with diverse groups of friends, Jesuit companions, clergy in San Salvador and his dear mentor Archbishop Chávez y González. He remembered them and wanted to be remembered as well.

Sought out by many, Rutilio was respected and loved by the archdiocesan clergy and religious men and women. He was often asked to give retreats, sermons, workshops, courses, and to serve on numerous archdiocesan commissions. His work in "rural ministry" had caught the attention of those he met during his years at Lumen Vitae and IPLA. While his educational opportunities brought him into contact with men and women across the globe, his pastoral experiment and experiences in the parish of Our Lord of Mercies in Aguilares ushered in a new approach to evangelization.

Nurtured by the proceedings of the Second Vatican Council and Medellín, Rutilio directly benefitted from the spirit of renewal that was sweeping across Latin America. In fact, the type of pastoral ministry that was happening in El Salvador was also being exercised in the United States. Hispanic Catholics in the U.S. were forming communities of faith (Base Christian Communities) and using the See-Judge-Act method in their efforts to assume their rightful place within the Church and U.S. society. The movement embraced the most marginalized groups among Hispanic Catholics, including farm workers and urban poor. With his wide contact, Rutilio was aware of what was happening among the campesino efforts of Hispanics in the U.S. In all of this, Rutilio Grande lived as a faithful son of the Second Vatican Council and of Medellín—one of the first-born.

ENDNOTES

1. Interview with Gaspar Romero, March 9, 2010. Spanish citation: *"No hay que protestar."*

2. Ibid.

3. Brockman, *Romero: A Life*, 40.

4. Ibid., 40.

5. Interview with Gaspar Romero, March 9, 2010.

6. Brockman, *Romero: A Life*, 40.

7. Interview with Gaspar Romero, March 9, 2010.

8. Delgado. *Óscar Romero Biografía*, 41.

9. CEE, CCR, 44. See Delgado, *Óscar A. Romero Biografía*, 43.

10. Ibid., 44. See also Maier, *Monseñor Romero: Maestro de Espiritualidad*, 34.

11. Delgado, *Óscar A. Romero Biografía*, 44.

12. Letter from Rutilio Grande to Provincial Francisco Estrada, July 25, 1970 (APCSJ). Spanish citation: *"He estado sometido a presiones por muchos lados, y eso desde que comenzaron los preparativos de la Consecración de Monseñor Romero."*

13. Letter from Archbishop Romero to Rutilio Grande on June 22, 1972 (APCSJ). Spanish citation: *'...que ese mismo día tuve una reunión en la Basílica donde se conserva el altar de aquella inolvidable concelebración...y he recordado con nuevos sentimientos de gratitud y cariño todas las finezas, actividades y sacrificios que Ud. se impuso junto con los buenos amigos seglares para lograr aquella inolvidable liturgia en la que Ud. fue el alma."*

14. Delgado, *Óscar A. Romero Biografía*, 48.

15. Ibid., 49.

16. Brockman, *Romero: A Life*, 44.

17. Delgado, *Óscar A. Romero Biografía*, 49.

18. Ibid., 49.

19. Ibid., 40, 104; See: Zacarías Diez and Juan Macho, *"En Santiago de María Me Topé Con La Miseria" Dos Años de la Vida de Monseñor Romero (1975-1976)*. There is no publisher or date of publication cited. The authors are members of the Passionist community who ministered in Santiago de María, El Salvador during the two years that Romero served in this diocese. It is possible to assume that this is a publication supported by the Passionist community. The title begins with words spoken by Monseñor Romero as he confronts the stark poverty of the diocese. It is a significant work on Romero since it specifically addresses

the two years preceding Romero's appointment in San Salvador and contains excerpts from key documents as well as testimonies from those who knew Romero during this time. According to the authors, the two years that Romero spent in Santiago de María were critical in his evolving transformation.

20. Brockman, *Romero: A Life*, 53.

21. Ibid., 58.

22. Carranza, *Romero-Rutilio Vidas Encontradas*, 39.

23. Delgado, *Óscar A. Romero Biografía*, 63.

24. Diez and Macho, 59-141. This section is rich with letters and testimonies of the exchanges that occurred between Romero, the President of El Salvador, the Passionist Provincial and other members of the diocesan community.

25. Ibid., 80-86.

26. Ibid., 128-29.

27. Interview with Gaspar Romero, March 9, 2010.

28. Delgado, *Óscar A. Romero Biografía*, 70.

29. Carranza, *Romero-Rutilio Vidas Encontradas*, 45. Spanish citation: "*Hay que ayudar al nuevo arzobispo, aunque no sea el que más nos guste. No podemos dejarle solo en estos momentos.*"

30. Ibid., 71.

31. Carranza, *Una Luz Grande Nos Brilló*, 3. Also: In an interview with Dina Elizabeth Mejia (July 10, 2014) she shared how as a young girl, Father Grande often encouraged her through moments of discouragement. Today as a mother of a young teenage girl, she is motivated by Grande's example.

32. *Orientación*, December 6-12, 1965 (APCSJ).

33. Interview with Octavio Cruz, May 12, 2014.

34. Interview with Gregorio Landaverde, May 5, 2014.

35. Ibid.

36. Interview with Octavio Cruz May 12, 2014.

37. Interviews: Octavio Cruz, May 12, 2014; Rutilio Sánchez July 1, 2014.

38. Interviews: Octavio Cruz, May 12, 2014; Gregorio Landaverde, Rutilio Sánchez July 1, 2014.

39. Interview with Benito Tovar, July 21, 2015.

40. Ibid.

41. Interview with Rutilio Sánchez July 1, 2014.

42. Interview with Gregorio Landaverde, May 5, 2014.

43. Interview with Benito Tovar, July 21, 2015.

44. Carranza, *Una Luz Grande Nos Brilló*, 27.

45. Letter from Rutilio Grande to Jesuit Provincial, November 30, 1969 (APCSJ).

46. Interview with Miguel Ventura, July 6, 2014.

47. Carranza, *Romero-Rutilio Vidas Encontradas*, 19.

48. Evaluation letter, May 12, 1976, anonymous (APCSJ).

49. Letter to Jaime Vera Fajardo from Rutilio Grande, April 9, 1972 (APCSJ).

50. Letter to Rutilio Grande from Alfonso López Trujillo, December 22, 1975 (APCSJ). Spanish citation: "*Sigo, con mucha alegría sus trabajos y lo que haces allí para despertar entusiasmo. Iré, Dios mediante, hacia el 10 de Febrero, a la Asamblea Episcopal. Ojalá tenga el gusto de verlo.*"

51. Letter to Rutilio Grande from Segundo Galilea, May 22, 1973 (APCSJ).

52. Letter to Rutilio Grande from Rodrigo (no surname included), Mexico, D.F., January 26, 1974 (APCSJ).

53. Letter from Provincial Miguel Francisco Estrada, SJ to Rutilio Grande in IPLA, March 10, 1972 (APCSJ). Spanish citation: "*Quisiera, Rutilio, que fueras pensando en esta empresa. No es nada fácil, pero los interesados lo han pedido y creo que podríamos contar además con la colaboración de otros SJ. Y no SJ. Peritos en pastoral, liturgia, sacramentos etc. Así pues, conviene ir proyectando un equipo que después puede por naciones o por obras específicas ir mentalizando a los sujetos y poniendo al día nuestras actividades apostólicas. Te lo anuncio desde ahora para que tengas una visión en tu trabajo y puedas también enriquecerte con las experiencias que puedas confrontar por allí.*"

54. Letter from Rutilio Grande to Provincial Miguel Francisco Estrada, S.J., July 14, 1972 (APCSJ).

55. Letter from Rutilio Grande to Provincial (APCSJ). Spanish citation: "*He encomendado el asunto a Dios y lo he pensado: pero no me fió de mi mismo. Con la mayor sinceridad y sin tapujos me pongo en sus manos para que V.R. disponga y vea lo que me conviene. Iré gustoso al sitio que me señale la obediencia y si dispone que me quede aquí, aquí me quedaré tranquilo.*"

56. Carranza, *Una Luz Grande Nos Brilló*, 44-45.

57. Letter from Archbishop Chávez y González to Rutilio Grande, August 3, 1972 (APCSJ).

58. Interview with Eva del Carmen Menjivar, May 7, 2014.

59. Ibid. Spanish citation: "*Esas señoras pueden transmitir mucho de Dios y son las que nos han transmitido.*"

60. Interview with Don Manuel Quijano, July 3, 2014.

61. Maier, *Monseñor Romero*, 103. An extensive excerpt of the conversation between Romero and Jerez is included in this work.

62. Ibid., 104.

63. Letter from Rutilio Grande to Flavio Grande, February 19, 1972. Spanish citation: "*Me alegro de las buenas noticias de El Paisnal. Todo se debe a una carta que entregué personalmente al Señor Arzobispo, cuando me fuí a despedir de él. En esa carta le exponía en términos patéticos la situación del pueblo, necesitado desde hace tiempo de un buen sacerdote o de una comunidad de Monjitas y le exponía como iba a quedar abandonado con mi venida. Quiera Dios que todo se arregle.*"

MONS ROMER

Detail, photograph of mural entitled *P. Tilo y Mons. Romero: Profetas de Liberación* (Padre Tilo and Bishop Romero: Prophets of Liberation) in El Paisnal where Father Rutilio Grande was born.

CHAPTER 4

SPIRITUALITY

The 1960s and '70s saw tumultuous changes and political unrest across the globe. The era that saw the building of the Berlin Wall and the Cuban Missile crisis also witnessed the election of the first Catholic U.S. President, John F. Kennedy, as well as his assassination and that of his brother Robert and of Dr. Martin Luther King, Jr. The era was marked by the Vietnam War as well as the Civil Rights movement, animated by King and César Chávez struggling for the rights of marginalized African-Americans and Hispanic communities.

In El Salvador, unstable authoritarian governments continued to employ political repression to maintain power. Under the guise of combating communism, they violently repulsed the efforts of workers and peasants to gain their human and civil rights, engendering a brutal civil war that divided the Church as well as the society.

In 1962 Pope Saint John XXIII convened the Second Vatican Council to renew the Church in the context of the modern world. The Council highlighted the importance of culture in the vernacularization of the liturgy and in the promotion of greater lay participation in both ritual and church life. Following John XXIII's death on June 3, 1963, and the succession of Pope Paul VI, the Latin American Conference of Bishops (CELAM) in 1968 met in Medellín, Colombia, to discuss the implementation of the proceedings of the Second Vatican Council. The conclusions of Medellín acknowledged the overwhelming poverty in Latin America and the imperative for the Church to respond to the realities of people in the process of evangelization. In 1972 and 1977, U.S. Hispanic Catholics gathered on the national level to discuss their inclusion in the life of the Catholic Church.

This time of historical change and upheaval created the backdrop for the development of Romero and Grande's lives of prayer and personal spirituality. While external forces in their lives can be researched and noted, the mysterious relationship that each of these men had with God is impossible to determine or completely understand. Personal journals, correspondence, liturgical celebrations and sermons, as well as what people remember of them, provide a glimpse into their spiritual growth and life. This glimpse is, however, a limited portal into God's presence to them and their response.

Óscar Romero

People who knew Óscar Romero as a child remember him as a rather serious boy given to quiet moments of prayer in the village church. Romero credited his father as the source of his own spiritual foundation. His father had passed on to his son a love for the saints and a habit of praying before meals and upon retiring for the night. As a grieving seventeen year old, he wrote: "My father is dead! Only the memories remain, memories of my childhood—how you would pace the bedroom floor as my child's understanding memorized the Our Father, the Hail Mary, the Creed, the Hail Holy Queen, the commandments that your fatherly lips taught me..."[1]

Even as a child and throughout his seminary years with the Claretian Fathers, Romero liked to pray late at night, especially before the Blessed Sacrament, which became part of his daily practice. The tranquility of night allowed him to focus entirely on communicating with God, a routine that he maintained his entire life.[2]

Through the Ignatian tradition, Óscar considered fidelity to the Pope as indispensable in his pursuit of the priestly ideal. He embraced the salvific and redemptive mystery of the Eucharist as central to his priestly vocation. The daily celebration of Mass was not merely a priestly practice nor a sentimental ritual, but the cornerstone of his daily life.

Following the morning celebration of the Mass, he routinely recited the rosary throughout the day.[3] His profound devotion to the Blessed Mother was constant in his personal and pastoral life. As a priest, he linked the mysteries of the rosary to the sacrifice of the Mass, giving the Marian prayer an even deeper significance for him. Spiritual practices acquired in his years of seminary formation continued to structure and nourish his life.

In 1966, during the latter part of his time in San Miguel, Romero began a Spiritual Diary, which included his retreat notes. The writing begins on January 15, 1966, and concludes with a final entry on February 25, 1980, during his last retreat, just a few weeks before his death. The opening entry in 1966 is significant for him. Two years had gone by since his June 1964 retreat in Guadalajara, Mexico, following which he had neglected to set aside time for another. The postponed experience, however, became a time of great renewal for Romero. He noted: "At nighttime, on the evening of Wednesday, January 12, I have felt a profound joy when I meditated on God's mercy...[4] Hope must be for me a basic virtue since I have seen this confirmed with clear and moving evidence. God still loves me. Thank you Señor!!!"[5]

Intent on finding a way to reform his life and return to the spiritual practices that he deemed so important in his relationship with God, during this retreat Romero twice visited with a psychologist, Dr. Dárdano. His diary notes: "The doctor and my spiritual director orient the solution to my problem to two central challenges of my reform: to fortify my interior life and to seek out a protective environment. The doctor summarized my character [as]: compulsive, obsessive, perfectionist."[6] Throughout his life, as he struggled with the limitations of his character Romero regularly visited with Dr. Dárdano.

In one of his later spiritual entries, Romero noted:

> "Subconsciously many influences from home are transmitted to my current relationships and this explains certain timidity, fear of others, etc... Lack of human warmth, coolness toward others etc...I must educate myself with the conviction that the relationship of parents to children is no longer what should regulate my relationship between men who are equal—I must be more natural and spontaneous in my affection."[7]

For his entire life, Romero made daily efforts to overcome his human limitations. In his spiritual diary, he frequently expressed his desire to "overcome my dry and surly nature. Treat with kindness those who seek me out. Above all priests, seminarians, the poor, the sick...etc.."[8] Consistently, Romero sought spiritual assistance to deal with the personal challenges that he experienced, both spiritual and psychological.

Based on Dárdano's psychological assessment and that of his spiritual director, besides returning to a more ordered life of prayer, meditation, and examination of conscience, weekly confession, and monthly retreat, Romero resolved to improve his communication with others.[9] His notes reflect his constant effort to overcome his human limitations for love of God and others. Close friends and collaborators were aware of the quickness of his temper.[10] Sister Luz, superior of the hospital where Romero lived, knew him well: "Monseñor Romero was a person like any human being. He would also get angry when things were not done his way, he would scold strongly and respond harshly..."[11] Afterwards, however, he would apologize to the person whom he had offended. "My perfectionism takes away much of the human richness in my relationships. I should be more natural, not lose myself so much in details, but better cultivate friendship. It is better to be more humane and generous than to be demanding and curt in details that are not important."[12] He pursued this journey of conversion throughout his life.

In his retreat as preparation for his ordination as Auxiliary Bishop of San Salvador in June 1970, Romero's spiritual notes are very revealing. He savored "the sweetness and the intimacy with Jesus"[13] and he dedicated his episcopacy to the Sacred Heart of Jesus as his patron.[14] He longed to offer reparation to the wounded Heart that suffered from humanity's sin.[15] In addition, his retreat notes express deep ecstasy in his soul, an experience of God's mercy, grace, and peace. It was a moment of rebirth of his baptismal promises and his priesthood. Invoking the Holy Spirit, he prayed: "Come Lord! We are together, renew me, guide me, and open me to the new infusion of the Spirit. In my episcopacy it will be the Spirit that will give me tremendous new powers...I need to be faithful in seeking God's glory and the good of the Church."[16]

He also set forth in detail how he planned to live out his episcopal ministry. Carefully he outlined a series of resolutions that addressed three areas: 1) understanding of the Church and his episcopal duties; 2) practices to follow in pursuit of personal sanctity; and 3) development of a deeper dialogue with his brother bishops, clergy, laity, and religious, as well as with his family and with the poor.[17] He wishes to love the poor, loving them as images of Christ.[18] On martyrdom he noted: "Everyone should be willing to confess Christ before men and to follow him on the way of the cross, amidst the persecutions that are never lacking in the Church."[19]

Twenty-four items, consistent with the spiritual notes of his seminary years, comprised the list of practices to support his pursuit of personal sanctity. The list included penitential exercises to help him keep his sensuality in check, e.g., fasting, eating in moderation, wearing a hair shirt daily for thirty minutes, using the "discipline" on Fridays. He committed himself to the regular and devotional celebration of Mass and carefully prepared for his private confession and spiritual direction. He sought to be faithful in praying the breviary and in reciting the hours. He pledged to give attention to his daily responsibilities and tasks in an orderly manner. He noted practices that would address what he deemed personal "sacrilegious" behavior. He also listed certain precautions to avoid occasions of temptation.[20] Understanding that the duty of the Church was to be in touch with humanity,[21] he committed to pursuing "dialogue" with those around him and with those whose lives he touched. This task particularly challenged Romero, who struggled to overcome his introversion and shyness and his tendency to be obsessive, compulsive and a perfectionist.

After Romero was named bishop of Santiago de María, as he directed his pastoral energies toward promoting the sacramental life and to preaching, he noticed how the men and women of his diocese suffered at the hands of the wealthy coffee plantation owners, working long hours for meager pay with no place to sleep at the end of the day. Coming into direct contact with the reality of the poor, Romero began to grasp truths that would lead him implacably along the road of transformation that he so desired, as well as to a culmination that he could not then have imagined.

During those two years as bishop of Santiago de María, Romero began to identify with and to truly love the "crucified peoples" of his homeland. His love for the Eucharist became enfleshed in the suffering of the poor. In the faces of the poor and in their stories of appalling oppression and injustice, Romero's love for the Crucified Jesus and the Eucharist perceived a human identity.

On March 12, 1977, Romero was impelled another step forward toward the Crucified Jesus. His friend and priestly brother Rutilio Grande, S.J., along with two companions, was murdered en route to celebrate a Mass for the novena of St. Joseph, patron saint of his hometown of El Paisnal. For a month after the killing of Rutilio Grande, military forces occupied the parish church of Aguilares, scattering and desecrating the Eucharistic host.[22]

It was a time of great desolation and suffering for the people of Aguilares. The inhabitants feared for their lives, and indeed the military killed many of them.[23] On June 19, 1977, to accompany the people and to re-consecrate the church, Archbishop Romero himself went to Aguilares. In his homily, he identified the terrorized people as "the image of the Pierced Holy One, of which the first reading speaks to us in a language prophetic and mysterious, but which represents Christ nailed to the cross and pierced through by the spear. It is the image of all the people that, like Aguilares, will be pierced, will be mistreated."[24] In the days and years following the murders, the violence and oppression of the poor and those committed to defend them escalated viciously.

Over the course of three years as Archbishop of San Salvador, Óscar Romero, the academic and administrator, received a powerful summons. Always a man rooted in a prayer life that was nurtured by family, formation, study, and grace; always a man striving for greater faithfulness and intimacy with God, now this man of prayer was confronted by the Christ of the poor. The human face of suffering evoked a galvanizing response in his soul.

In his sermon on Palm Sunday 1978, Romero began to use the phrase "crucified people." In his Good Friday homily, he asserted: "It is our tortured people—it is our people crucified, spat upon, and humiliated—that represents Our Lord Jesus Christ to give our difficult situation a sense of redemption."[25] Romero's love for Christ present in the Eucharist was now drawing him to Eucharistic presence of the "Crucified Christ" in the suffering people of El Salvador.

The "Crucified Christ" and the "Crucified people" of El Salvador became a constant focus of Romero's episcopal life. The image reappeared again and again in his homilies and in his pastoral letters. The increasing violence was "crucifying" the people of El Salvador, especially the poor. Tragically the death or disappearance of "priests, seminarians, students, campesinos, teachers, workers, professionals, and intellectuals murdered for the faith in El Salvador"[26] became commonplace.

As archbishop of the nation's capital, Romero embraced the responsibility to speak out against the violence and the abuse of power. His Sunday homilies, in the light of the Gospel, reflected upon the week's events of injustice and savagery. Romero believed that "besides reading the Bible, which is the Word of God, a Christian who is faithful to the word must also read the signs of the times, the events, to illuminate them through the word."[27] Because of his denunciation of the acts of terror and those who promoted it, he lost the support of his own brother bishops and of those political and wealthy allies who in the past had befriended him. He received repeated threats on his own life.

Given the ferociousness of the violence confronted, he faced the reality of his own death. He had often reflected on the theme of death in his annual retreats. But by his final retreat on February 25, 1980, he had become more convinced that his actual death was imminent and inevitable. Earlier he had thought to go to Guatemala for the retreat, but the intensifying violence discouraged the plan. As his retreat notes reveal, he sought God's will, and he examined his life and responsibilities as the pastor of a suffering country. He prayed that God would allow him to be so transparent that His love, justice and truth would be revealed. At the same time, he feared the violence that he might have to suffer. In that retreat week itself, he had been warned of a series of threats to his life. He asked God to grant him serenity, perseverance and humility even as he struggled with his own weakness and temptation to vanity.[28]

During the retreat he shared his examination of conscience with his confessor, who reminded him of the importance of one's interior disposition and counseled him against scrupulosity. He encouraged

Romero to adopt a plan for his spiritual life but not to become enslaved to it. With his confessor, he shared his fears for his life and the difficulty he had in accepting a violent death. From His confessor he received deep comfort. With the grace of his retreat, Romero was able to entrust himself fully to God and to whatever lay ahead.

Perspective

Faithfulness marked Romero's life of prayer and to the spiritual practices that he had espoused. Above all else, he strove to live the Gospel and to seek union with God. His journey toward God was lifelong, and each step part of the essential, enduring elements of his Christian transformation.

From a contemporary perspective some of Romero's spiritual practices may be problematic. According to his own spiritual notes, he used the discipline and the hair shirt. After his death, his Vicar General, Monseñor Urioste, found a discipline and a mortification anklet inside the drawer of his bedside stand.[29] Physical mortifications seem somewhat "old-fashioned," at odds with the image of the robust spirituality associated with the image of Romero as the courageous shepherd, lover and defender of the poor. But Romero's spiritual notes also reveal his worry about the dangers of his "sensuality." He adopted these practices to strengthen his resistance to the temptations of the flesh. What was the value or efficacy of these spiritual practices for the Romero of El Salvador? Are they merely a form of an old-fashioned spirituality, or is there more to be seen in them?

Perhaps a key to the question is found in the plea that Romero addressed to the clergy when he was Bishop of Santiago de María: "Help me to see clearly."[30] Throughout his life, Romero struggled to know the truth and live it. The circumstances of his life and his tendency to scrupulosity may have developed in him an exaggerated fidelity to dogma as truth. He loved the Church and the Pope, and from his days in the seminary, it was extremely important for him to uphold papal authority and the teachings of the Church. At the same time, he was an intelligent and educated man who appealed to reason to affirm authenticity in the Church and in his priestly ministry.[31]

In a steady and thoughtful manner, he pursued what he thought to be the truth. But the unfolding reality of El Salvador confronted him with new dimensions of truth. When he encountered the coffee workers in Santiago de María, he recognized the truth of the poor. The overwhelming misery and the deadly consequences of poverty, especially as suffered by the innocent children, opened his eyes to more truths. He perceived "The face of Christ amid the bags and baskets of those who pick coffee…The face of Christ dying of hunger amid the children who have nothing to eat."[32]

Burdened with a tendency to solitary introspection, Romero had been accustomed to making decisions alone, the direction always following from prayer and study.[33] Yet, gradually he learned the importance of seeking insight from others. From the accounts of those who knew him, he was always willing to enter into dialectical relationships with others, regardless of their social position or economic status.[34]

In the light of God's word, he examined the events of each week in violence-torn El Salvador. From that standpoint he announced and denounced the abuses that the people were suffering. Romero came to look toward the lived reality of the people of El Salvador, especially the poor, to learn how to live a committed Christian life. In witnessing the deaths of countless Salvadorans, he painfully learned what it meant to live the truth of the Gospel.

Monseñor Ricardo Urioste, his Vicar General, compared Romero to the blind man in the Gospel (MARK 8:22-26) whose sight is restored by Jesus. As the blind man's sight returns, he first sees men who appear to be like trees.[35] Later, the afflicted man realizes that what he is looking at are not trees but men.

Such was the gradual journey along the road of truth that Romero walked. His life of prayer helped him to see things increasingly more clearly: "We want a church that is elbow to elbow (*codo a codo*) with the poor people of El Salvador; and we realize that it is in this act of drawing near to the poor, that we discover the true face of the Suffering Servant of Yahweh."[36]

Engendered in his earliest life and brought to fullness at the moment of his martyrdom, three compelling forces fashioned the noble man who *became* Óscar Romero: his life of prayer, his search for the truth, and his commitment to the poor and marginalized.

Rutilio Grande

Life in El Paisnal was the cradle of Rutilio Grande's spiritual life. His devout paternal grandmother Francisca shaped his religiosity, teaching him the traditional prayers and how to recite the rosary.[37] Immersed in the religious feasts and processions of the town,[38] it is easy to imagine the boy Rutilio delighting in the days leading up to the community's patronal feast, going with his grandmother to prepare the church for the nine consecutive days of the novena held in honor of St. Joseph, joining the entire populace on March 19 for the mass, and reveling in the fireworks, games, and the shared food that followed. The townspeople embraced the boy's youthful spirituality in their awareness of the bells that signaled young Rutilio's daily "mass" with his cousins and friends.

Needless to say, El Paisnal nourished in this child a deep and abiding love for the popular expressions of the faith of his community, a piety fundamentally rooted in the reality of that humble community. Years later, a Jesuit companion, noted, "He [Rutilio] is also profoundly religious and respectful of popular religion."[39] The seminarians whom he formed recalled how Rutilio made it a point to take them to the outlying towns for the religious celebrations of the people.[40] For Rutilio, El Paisnal was the wellspring of piety and popular religious practices not only as a child but also as an adult.

Leaving his native town to enter the seminary removed Rutilio from the immediacy of that experience of popular religious practices. At the same time, religious piety, similar to that which he had developed in his home, constituted one of the important dimensions of formation in the minor seminary at San Salvador. According to Cardenal: "theoretically by piety it was understood the disposition of the soul that was to boost the performance of the duties that the rational creature owes to its creator that found expression through personal and devout worship."[41] The seminary required both punctuality in carrying out pious acts and also frequency of visits to the chapel, as these were considered to be central to the development of piety.[42]

The framework of piety structured the day of the seminarian. Each morning Rutilio rose and recited prayers aloud while he dressed, then went to chapel to meditate for a half hour, and followed this by Mass. His spiritual director assigned fifteen minutes of spiritual reading and encouraged visits to the chapel after meals and whenever possible. Prayers during the day included recitation of the rosary, three pauses for the Angelus, prayers before and after class, with night prayers concluding the day.[43]

At the beginning of each year Rutilio and his seminary classmates made an eight-day Ignatian retreat. During the school year, each seminarian regularly went to his spiritual director for confession. Seminarians learned Gregorian chant and how to serve at the altar. Celebrating the birthdays of the local bishops promoted reverence for ecclesiastical authority.[44] The pious practices inculcated in the minor seminary undoubtedly influenced Rutilio's personal relationship with God.

When the young seminarian from El Paisnal discontinued his formation at the archdiocesan seminary, he joined the Society of Jesus in 1945. The life of the Jesuit community led him to embrace Ignatian spirituality more fully. The Spiritual Exercises, daily exams, and retreats in the Ignatian spirit became a regular part of Rutilio's spiritual practice.

In the ensuing years, Rutilio occasionally disclosed his interior life and relationship with God in his communications with his provincials, brother Jesuits and close friends. Rutilio's own words provide a glimpse into his soul. During significant moments of his life, he wrote short spiritual notes that revealed his love for God and his desire to give himself over to God without reserve.

A couple of years after his first psychological crisis, when he had been sent to Oña, Spain, to continue his Jesuit formation, he wrote to Agustín Bariáin, his Vice-Provincial: "At the beginning of the school year, the Lord granted me a great grace: some spiritual exercises that touched me deeply. Father Agacino directed them and I catalog them among the best I've done in my life; I would almost say the best...

I believe that I have come to stabilize my method of prayer and I have settled on a system of spiritual life, [that is] unifying, simple and which accommodates my way of being.[45] Every day I ask Our Lord with fervor for the gift of good health and I believe that I also do my part."[46]

His prayers often asked God for health and a quiet acceptance of his debilitated condition. Although as a young enthusiastic novice Rutilio had prayed to God to be given a heavy cross to bear, he never imagined that it would be his psychological condition. Acutely aware of the weakness of his nervous system, he recognized it as the cross that he had prayed for. At the same time, he was fully confident that he would manage because not only would God help him but also God would give him the optimism to trust in that support. Wholeheartedly embracing the cross of his psychological fragility, Rutilio accepted it without complaining or brandishing its consequences. He believed that his quiet acceptance pleased God.[47]

During his Tertianship in Cordova, Spain in 1962, Rutilio made a retreat that afforded great consolation and insight. Expressing a deep faith in God's providence, he accepted, with all his human limitations that God had chosen him just the way he is. He acknowledged that he, of course, must make the effort to better himself, but not become someone other than himself. Given that his only intention would be to promote God's glory, all would be well: the only thing that matters is love.

In his retreat reflections, Grande's desire was to encounter God by seeking true spiritual poverty and truly depending on God in all things. He contemplated the mystery of God's plans: that the Kingdom of God will be realized on earth in ways that Rutilio can neither foresee nor necessarily understand. The final triumph would be that of Christ, when all will be restored and God's plans realized.

All his reflections from retreat show him aspiring to realize the third way of Ignatian humility. He prays to be able to imitate Jesus in all things, to empty himself as Jesus did even to the point of being mistreated and dishonored. His retreat notes end with the insight and resolve: "Christ has given me all. I must return it in serving my brothers—first those at home—in order that God's mystery in them be realized.[48]

During his retreats over the next three years, several themes recur. The priority of God's providence was a constant. In his 1963 retreat, Rutilio acknowledged, "God's providence is everything. [I have] feelings of being in his hands like a child in his Father's: peace for the present and a remedy against future fears."[49] Grande believed that God had chosen him fully without condition, and he must continue to seek total spiritual poverty in every aspect of life. Another recurring theme is that of the third way of humility that Rutilio believed as fundamental to fully living the Jesuit ideals.

Throughout his retreats from 1963 to 1966, new insights surfaced, such as the need for penance and the sacrifices even of things that of themselves are good. Corporal mortification had at one time been accepted as a practice within religious orders. Although for a very short time Rutilio tried using a *cilice*—a spiked chain that was worn around the upper thigh—he soon realized that his health could not sustain this penitential method. He made resolutions to enliven his spiritual life by giving special attention to the breviary and prayers to the Blessed Mother.[50] He resolved to allow more time for prayer, especially the expression of gratitude. In his retreat for final vows, Grande wrote: "God is my Father. He has created me solely out of love. I want to feel in all my life as a child in the hands of his Father."[51]

Rutilio did not consider the brooding over failures to be either effective or helpful for the Kingdom of God. He wanted to follow Christ's example in all his activities. He especially desired to embrace the poor as his brothers and not simply to see Jesus Christ in them: to embrace the humanity of the poor for who they are. Gratitude for the reality of Jesus' love permeated his life. In the face of anything that can happen in life, Rutilio committed himself to accept everything for love of Jesus.[52] All else may fail except for the love Jesus has for him.

During his 1964 retreat in Brussels he reflected on how much Christ had done for him, Christ who loved him unconditionally, who invited him to a greater understanding of the significance of the Incarnation. His reflections returned him to the dogma of the Communion of Saints and the concept of solidarity.[53]

The following year, during his newly assigned ministry at the seminary of San José de La Montaña, notes from the spiritual exercises reveal him to have been praying for God's encouragement, asking for the grace of light and strength. He begs for a palpable experience of God and that his ears might be opened, that he might contribute to the edification of the Mystical Body of Christ.[54]

Despite his need for God's consoling reassurance, he wrote that in many ways he feels like a multi-millionaire, showered with abundant graces: "God's work in my vocation is marvelous. [God is] sorting out the difficulties and holding me tightly in his grip. Thank you. Lord, the daily petition for perseverance is also a thanksgiving in itself."[55]

Determined to place all his confidence in God, Rutilio wanted to avoid the temptations of either looking for human satisfaction or seeking the esteem of others. He resolved to carry out his vow of obedience and to look for God in everything, a sentiment that recurs in his future retreats.

Through his retreat reflections, Rutilio came to the conclusion that he needed to fight against personal timidity and cowardice. If he was unable to control these feelings, given his temperament, then he might stop doing what God wanted of him.[56] He determined that the way of handling this temptation was to work against being a perfectionist, but rather to be open to learning in the doing. Preparation for a task is necessary, but not to excess.

After years of the spiritual exercises, Grande concluded that ultimately love is the only thing that matters. "Christ, always waits—he is there to always accompany—to always receive with open arms and hearts; to always listen; to always understand; to always forgive without fear; to always console. God on His part always fulfills. He is always open, never tires, never fails, never abandons in even the smallest infidelity."[57]

One's interior life is mysterious and only fully known by the person themselves and God. While Rutilio Grande's retreat notes offer an intimate glance into his spiritual life, other reflections written over approximately five years offer further glimpses into his life of prayer and his relationship with God.

In 1968, when Segundo Azcue, the Jesuit Provincial, elicited the community's input on the nature of prayer as practiced among the members of the Society of Jesus, Rutilio responded with a thoughtful letter. He offered ways that could strengthen the experience of prayer among his Jesuit brothers. From his perspective, the dynamic interplay between the apostolic and pastoral life was essential. Engagement in the apostolic life nourishes the life of prayer within the community, and, as a result, the apostolic-pastoral life assumes more vitality and realism.

In analyzing the contemporary condition of the apostolic works of Jesuits, Rutilio observed that they more closely resembled businesses that could be run by anyone. The apostolic works had become islands of activity disconnected from the social, moral and religious reality that surrounded them. He noted that the Jesuits did not project attention toward the world, contrary to the genuine spirit of the Constitutions of the Society of Jesus that was characterized by a willingness to accept risk and to seek new perspectives.[58] In a context that lacks the idealism and a profound sense of Jesuits' religious vocation, "prayer does not find a suitable place for its sustenance nor can we feel its connection with our daily life."[59]

To revitalize their life of prayer, Rutilio recommended moving away from individualism to living truly as a community. He suggested that community members gather in small reflection groups using the method of See, Judge, and Act to facilitate authentic life reviews. Lastly, Grande underscored the importance of looking for ways to saturate Jesuit apostolic endeavors with pastoral zeal.[60] All of these considerations would renew the life of prayer for the Jesuits.

For Rutilio, liturgy itself was a deep source of prayer. In his genuine love for the celebration of liturgy no detail was insignificant. Even with all his many ministerial obligations, he always found time to prayerfully prepare liturgy. His friends saw the care that he gave to the preparation of both the Eucharist and other liturgical celebrations. A few of his reflections on Holy Week demonstrate his deep devotion. One Good Friday reflection directed to Our Lady of Solitude—*Soledad*—is beautifully expressive and poetic.

They are gone, Mother, they have left you alone.
Alone with the child in your arms like as on that
night in Bethlehem! They are all gone:
Soldiers and Pharisees,
Merchants and daughters of Jerusalem,
Apostles…
All the rabble
All of humanity
Gone down to Jerusalem
With them we have all gone.
For ourselves as well
Good Friday
But a moment…
Afterwards we return to the same.
Above, at the top of the hill,
You are alone, Mother.
Alone with your Son in your arms
The rest of us
Have returned to town.[61]

In this evocative elegy to *Soledad*, Rutilio placed himself in the presence of the Sorrowing Mother left alone with her child in her arms. Surely Rutilio's personal experiences of abandonment, illness, and struggle infused his empathy with *Soledad*, as well as with suffering mothers throughout the world.

Over the years, the child of El Paisnal's love for God matured, and as an adult the prayer of the Church profoundly influenced his spirituality. Another important dimension of Rutilio Grande's spirituality, however, was the expressions of faith and religiosity in the lives of the people of the towns and countryside.[62] He expressed his affinity with the common folk in a Holy Thursday letter written to his team members in Aguilares:

"I am writing this letter seated beneath a beautiful *amate* tree, while pigs wander around, while the roosters sing, and while I see the pale faces of children with their extended stomachs.

It is 4:30 in the afternoon and shortly the people will

be arriving in procession from the diverse farmhouses for the celebration of the Word of God with these humble people who are also children of God and our brothers like the ones in Aguilares and like men and [women] from anywhere in the world.

On Sunday the 14th, the Feast of the Resurrection, we will have a popular celebration: They will come with their music from the nearby hamlets, with joy…and some toys and much folklore."[63]

Rutilio rooted his matured spirituality and his innovative ministry in the popular faith of the people. In Aguilares, he insisted that the work of the team be shaped by the people's faith. Rutilio's exceptional gift in this area was evidenced in his transformation of traditional religious celebrations such as the Feast of the Corn (*La Fiesta del Maíz*), centering it not only in the celebration of Mary, the Mother of God, but also by extension including all Salvadoran women, especially women of the poor. Praising the value of rural (*peasant*) women as the perfect embodiment of "*nuestro pueblo* (our people)" he called attention not only to women, but also to the sacredness of corn as the primary sustenance of the land. For the celebration, he invited each community to collectively bring food made from corn to be shared in the festivity. Each community was asked to present a creative representation of the many uses of corn, for example, a song in praise of corn or a decoration accenting its natural beauty. In addition, each community would present a woman as its godmother selected for her service and efforts on behalf of the community. Rutilio put the finishing touch to the celebration by delivering a sermon proclaiming Mary's Magnificat and extolling the importance of women and their communities.[64]

Another noteworthy dimension of Rutilio's liturgical gifts were the links that he drew between the popular expressions of the people's faith and the gospel call to transform existing realities. On an occasion in Apopa where, in assembly, clergy and laity were protesting the expulsion from El Salvador of Fr. Mario Bernal, the archdiocesan vicariate had designated Rutilio to be the spokesperson for the liturgical convocation. In the celebration of the Eucharist, Grande demonstrated his awareness of how faith needed to respond to the actual needs of the people; rather than refer to gathering as a protest march, he called it a "manifestation of faith."[65] For Rutilio, life was the demonstration of faith.

Perspective

At a time when the world poised for great changes, Rutilio Grande had been born in one of the smallest town of El Salvador. He was part of the popular religiosity and the piety of El Paisnal with all its rural reality; it shaped his childhood religiosity. It was natural for him to "celebrate" Mass as part of his childhood activity. By all accounts, the people accepted it as part of the town's rhythm of life. And, in fact, the life of the town often revolved around religious festivities and the local parish church. Life of the town square merged with the liturgical rituals that took place inside the church. All this nourished Rutilio's life of prayer and his nascent relationship with God. His early encounters with God through ritual and town life laid the foundation of his later prayer and spirituality.

The years in the seminary imbued with Ignatian spirituality gave structure to the devotional practices that were part of Rutilio's spiritual life. Once he entered the Society of Jesus, he was immersed in the Spiritual Exercises, daily exams, and retreats: great sources of spiritual nourishment that strengthened both his relationship with God and his Jesuit vocation. In fact, being a Jesuit was one of Grande's greatest joys. He loved his priestly vocation and he loved being part of the Society of Jesus.

As one whose grandmother had inducted him into the liturgical life of the town, one of this priest's great loves was the celebration of the liturgy. The seminarians that he taught witnessed to the care that he invested in the preparation of liturgy. In their shared memories of him, his students recalled that liturgy was given more attention during Rutilio's tenure in San José de la Montaña. A procession marked the beginning of the Archdiocesan Pastoral Week. The Missions that were carried out in the towns visited by the seminarians during the summer centered around the liturgy. As the prefect and professor of pastoral and liturgical ministry, Rutilio organized the celebration of the patronal feast of *El Divino Salvador*, producing a liturgical masterpiece. In the midst of such a joyful event that included an impressive procession, he always emphasized to the seminarians that what they were ritualizing was a "manifestation of faith" and not just a procession.

The seminarians regularly participated in the myriad of popular liturgical celebrations of the surrounding towns. Even after Rutilio left his ministry at the seminary and assumed the pastoral leadership of the parish of Aguilares, he invited the students to attend the ordination of fellow classmates. One of Grande's team members, Salvador Carranza, wrote while recalling the ordination of three Jesuits, "The celebration was so well attended that the church and its surroundings was [sic] brimming with campesinos. It was so solemn and popular as only Rutilio knew how to prepare them. After noon, when everything had been shared, in the courtyard of the convent, songs, and the people's party continued..."[66]

Rutilio meticulously prepared and outlined every ritual in writing. Each step of the Mass followed clear instructions on how it was to be done, and by whom. Those who knew him well, or who worked with him, greatly understood that he would tolerate neither a lack of preparation of the liturgy nor any disregard for the sacred vessels. This was, in fact, a trait that he shared with Romero, and probably why Romero asked Grande to organize his episcopal ordination as Auxiliary bishop of San Salvador in 1970. Some interpreted Rutilio's attitude toward liturgy as excessive. But, it is easy to surmise that for him, the attention given to liturgical rituals was motivated by the fact that participation in liturgy led to union with God. That was the heart of the matter.

As evident in his transformation of the "*Fiesta del Maíz* (The Festival of the Corn)," the mode through which the common people expressed their faith inspired Rutilio. From a purely cultural festival it became rich with religious significance. He linked prayer, popular expressions of faith, and liturgy to the contemporary world that Salvadorans were living. He saw salvation history in the context of the modern world, reinforcing the gospel imperative that prayer and good works be united.

In another instance, Rutilio had been accompanying a group of El

Paisnal men who were devoted to the Adoration of the Eucharist. He hoped that after the men received more religious formation that they would eventually begin a cooperative as the expression of their deep devotion to the Eucharist. In a letter to Fr. Romeo Maeda asking him to provide the members of the Adoration of the Eucharist with technical training on how to form a co-op, Rutilio wrote:

> "Well, these devotees of the [Blessed Sacrament] already possess a communal mysticism; I want to convert them into leaders of evangelization... I hope with all my soul that a well-developed co-op, filled with an ardent Christian mysticism, centered on the Eucharist, will be the *palanca* (lever) for the transformation of the entire pueblo. The breaking of the Bread was from the beginning of the early Church the departure point and arrival for the Christian Revolution: the sense of community was lived with joy in the celebration of the Eucharist itself. From the celebration one would leave with a commitment filled with a communal mysticism, ready to live a healthy community life."[67]

Grande had once made a similar observation to the Jesuit Provincial regarding Jesuit prayer. From his perspective, it was essential to recover the value of the dynamic interplay between the apostolic and pastoral life. Engagement in the apostolic life would in turn nourish the life of prayer within the Jesuit community.[68] Again in this instance, he recommended that the confraternity follow the See-Judge-Act method that was so prevalent among the Basic Christian Communities in Latin America and among Hispanic Catholics in the United States.

As one of his Jesuit brothers said of him: "He is a man of prayer. He feels with the Church and is well aware of the feeling of the Latin American Church...he is sensitive in nature...rather contemplative, of much imagination and picturesque expression.[69] Interestingly Monseñor Ricardo Urioste wrote something very similar about Archbishop Romero: "He [Romero] was very much in contact with God, and steeped in God...He felt God within himself at all times and in all circumstances."[70] The same might be said of Rutilio Grande. He was a man of prayer. There were several loves in his life. He loved God, the Church, the Salvadoran people—especially the poor—and the Society of Jesus: they shaped and informed his prayer and his spiritual character.

To speak definitively of the spiritual life of martyrs is a challenging and illusive task. No one can ascertain exactly the dynamic relationship between a person and God. These two noble men both carried that relationship to the ultimate surrender of life.

Both of these outstanding men came from humble beginnings in twentieth-century El Salvador. From an early age they developed lives of prayer and offered the days of their lives as their gift to God. Their priestly formation, while engendering spiritual growth and including higher studies, saw them embark on very different ministerial paths. Romero spent decades in administrative service while Rutilio always found a way to walk among the common people.

Now they are gone and the mystery of their spiritualities—the depth and authenticity and richness of their spiritual lives—can only be glimpsed through the legacy of their actions and their words.

ENDNOTES

1. Delgado, *Óscar A. Romero Biografía*, 11. Spanish citation: "*Solo quedan los recuerdos, recuerdos de la infancia—como te paseabas en el dormitorio, mi entendimiento de niño va grabando el Padre Nuestro, El Ave María, el Credo, la Salve, los mandamientos que tus labios de padre me van enseñando...*"

2. Maier, *Monseñor Romero: Maestro de Espiritualidad*, 27.

3. Brockman, *Romero: A Life*, 74.

4. CEE, CCR; also: Copy of CEE in CMR. Spanish citation: "*He sentido este miércoles 12 Enero por la noche una alegría profunda cuando medito en la misericordia de Dios.*"

5. Ibid., 67-68.

6. Ibid., 5.

7. Ibid., 66. Spanish citation: "*Influyen muchos subconscientes del hogar trasladados a mis relaciones actuales y esto explica cierta timidez, temor a los otros, etc. Falta de calor humano, sequedad de trato, etc. Debo educarme con la convicción de que aquella figura de padres a hijos ya no es la que debe regular las relaciones entre hombres iguales. –Debo ser más natural y espontáneo en el cariño.*"

8. Ibid., 7. Spanish citation: "*Vencer mi natural seco y hosco. Atender con amabilidad a quien me busca. Sobre todo con sacerdotes, seminaristas, pobres, enfermos...etc.*"

9. Ibid., 5.

10. Ricardo Urioste "*Y Su Sentir Con La Iglesia*" in Sobrino et al., 60.

11. Ibid., "*Madre Luz de la Cueva: Testimonios,*" 123.

12. CEE, CCR, 67-68. Spanish citation: "*El perfeccionismo hace perder mucha riqueza humana en mis relaciones. Debo ser más natural. No perderme tanto en detalles y cultivar mejor la amistad. –Mas vale ser más humano y generoso que ser exigente y roñoso en detalles sin importancia.*"

13. CEE, 44. See: Delgado, *Óscar A. Romero Biografía,* 43.

14. Ibid., 44. See also Maier, *Maestro de Espiritualidad,* 34.

15. Delgado, *Óscar A. Romero Biografía,* 44.

16. CEE, CCR, 45. Additional working copy at CMR.

17. Ibid., 51.

18. Ibid., 56.

19. Ibid., 50.

20. Ibid., 52.

21. Ibid., 55.

22. Maier, *Maestro de Espiritualidad,* 50.

23. Erdozain, *Archbishop Romero: Martyr of Salvador,* 25.

24. Maier, *Maestro de Espiritualidad,* 137.

25. Ibid., 138.

26. Sobrino, *Spirituality of Liberation,* 153.

27. Hodgson, *Through the Year With Óscar Romero,* 17.

28. CEE, 301. See also: Delgado, *Óscar A. Romero Biografía.*

29. Ricardo Urioste "*Monseñor Romero y su sentir con la Iglesia*" in Sobrino et al, *La Espiritualidad de Monseñor Romero: Servir Con La Iglesia,* 73.

30. Maier, *Maestro de Espiritualidad,* 40.

31. Erdozain, *Archbishop Romero: Martyr of Salvador,* 7.

32. Hodgson, *Through the Year With Óscar Romero,* 79.

33. Erdozain, *Archbishop Romero: Martyr of Salvador,* 7.

34. Ibid., 29.

35. Ricardo Urioste "*Monseñor y su sentir con la Iglesia*" in Sobrino, et al, 69.

36. Ibid., 72.

37. Letter to Archbishop Chávez y González from Rutilio Grande, January 11, 1976 (APCSJ).

38. Carranza, *Romero-Rutilio Vidas Encontradas*, 43.

39. Fragment of evaluation by Jesuits, no date noted.

40. Interviews with Gregorio Landaverde, May 8, 2014; Octavio Cruz, May 12, 2014; Rutilio Sánchez, July 1, 2014; Miguel Ventura, July 6, 2014; Benito Tovar, July 21, 2015.

41. Rodolfo Cardenal, *Historia de una Esperanza, Vida de Rutilio Grande*, 36. Spanish citation: "*teóricamente por piedad se entendía una disposición del alma que debía impulsar al cumplimiento de los deberes que la creatura racional tiene para con su creador, al que tribute culto filial y devoto.*"

42. Ibid., 36.

43. See Cardenal, *Historia de una Esperanza, Vida de Rutilio Grande*, 36-37.

44. Ibid., 37.

45. Letter from Rutilio Grande to Agustín Bariáin, S.J. December 4, 1955 (APCSJ). Spanish citation: "*El Señor me concedió, al comenzar el curso, una gracia muy grande: unos Ejercicios que me llegaron muy a lo hondo. Nos los dio el P. Agacino y yo los catálogo entre los mejores que he hecho en mi vida; casi diría, los mejores…Creo que he llegado a estabilizar mi método de oración y me he asentado en un sistema de vida espiritual, unificador, sencillo y acomodado a mi modo de ser.*"

46. Ibid. Spanish citation: "*Todos los días le pido al Señor con especial empeño el don de una buena salud y creo que de mi parte también pongo los medios.*"

47. Ibid.

48. Retreat Notes, Rutilio Grande, SJ, 1962 (APCSJ).

49. Ibid., 1963.

50. Ibid., 1962.

51. Ibid., 1963. Spanish citation: *Dios es mi Padre. Me ha creado solo por amor. Debería sentirme en toda mi vida así como un niño en manos de su Padre.*

52. Ibid.

53. Ibid.

54. Retreat Notes, Rutilio Grande, SJ, 1965 (APCSJ).

55. Ibid., 1965.

56. Ibid., 1966.

57. Ibid.

58. Letter from Rutilio Grande to Segundo Azcue, SJ, July 14, 1968 (APCSJ).

59. Ibid.

60. Ibid.

61. Rutilio Grande, in his own handwriting; Good Friday, no date (APCSJ).

62. Carranza, *Una Luz Grande Nos Brilló*, 47.

63. Rutilio Grande, SJ to Begnino Fernández and Jesús Ángel Bengoechea, April 9,

1974 (APCSJ).

64. Carranza, *Una Luz Grande Nos Brilló*, 66-67.

65. Idem, *Romero-Rutilio Vidas Encontradas*, 46.

66. Ibid., 43.

67. Letter from Rutilio Grande to Fr. Romeo Maeda, Aug. 25, 1970 (APCSJ). Spanish citation: "*Yo espero con toda mi alma que una cooperativa bien montada, con una mística de cristianismo al rojo vivo, en torno a la Eucaristía, será la palanca de transformación para todo el pueblo. La fracción del Pan, fue desde el comienzo de la Iglesia el punto de partida y de llegada de la Revolución Cristiana: se vivía con alegría el sentido comunitario en la misma celebración de la Eucaristía. De la celebración se salía con una mística de acción comunitaria, dispuestos a vivir un comunismo sano.*"

68. Letter from Rutilio Grande to Segundo Azcue, SJ, June 14, 1968 (APCSJ).

69. Evaluation of Grande by Jesuit brothers (APCSJ). Spanish citation: "*En suma, un carácter afectivo, secundario y poco activo, más bien contemplativo, de mucha imaginación y de pintoresca expresión.*"

70. Ricardo Urioste "*Monseñor y su sentir con la Iglesia*" in Sobrino et al, 61.

5

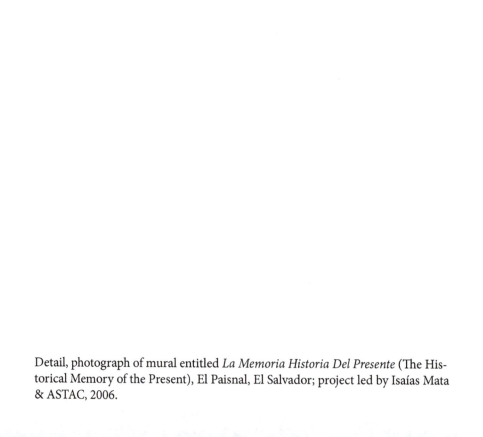

Detail, photograph of mural entitled *La Memoria Historia Del Presente* (The Historical Memory of the Present), El Paisnal, El Salvador; project led by Isaías Mata & ASTAC, 2006.

CHAPTER 5

THE POWER OF THE WORD

The decade of the 1970s continued to experience social and political unrest across the world. While armed conflict intensified in Cambodia and Vietnam, in the United States, the unpopularity of tens of thousands of Americans dying for an unclear cause eventually led to the end of U.S. involvement in Vietnam and Southeast Asia. Iranian militants took over the U.S. embassy in Tehran on November 4, 1979, holding fifty-two hostages for 444 days.

In El Salvador, political instability persisted. The fraudulent presidential election of Colonel Arturo A. Molina (1972-1977), whose installation was accepted by the United States, led to the formation of student resistance groups, and all political opposition was considered a communist threat to democracy.

Re-convoking the Second Vatican Council upon the death of John XXIII, Pope Paul VI (1963-1978) implemented its proceedings. He promoted dialogue with the world, the reform of canon law, the spread of social peace and justice throughout the world, and the unity of all Christians. As the Church in El Salvador distanced itself more from its earlier alliances with the government and the wealthy, the consciousness-raising effort taking place among the faithful Salvadoran Catholics was labeled "subversive." In the United States, however, Hispanic Catholics were assuming increasing ministerial leadership giving special attention to issues of justice.

Archbishop Óscar Romero

The art of communication manifested in many stages of Óscar Romero's life. Despite his natural inclination to shyness, from his early childhood he demonstrated an interest and a natural ability for public speaking. During his years in the minor seminary of San Miguel, in collaboration with his talented classmate, Rafael Valladares, Romero's gifts flourished. He wrote poems to the Sacred

Heart of Jesus and to the Blessed Mother under the title of Heart of Mary (*Corazón de María*), as well as poems expressing his idealization of the priesthood.[1]

On one occasion, while he was a seminarian, the local ordinary, Bishop Dueñas, held a contest for the best literary piece to be delivered to Pope Pius XI. The entries of both Valladares and Romero were selected and sent to the Pope to demonstrate the fine literary accomplishments of the seminary.[2] Writing projects in the seminary promoted Romero's literary development.

Early on, Romero started a file filled with ideas, anecdotes, and personal lecture notes for later use. It grew into a massive file of notes, ideas, and anecdotes that was found after his death. His habit of staying current on all the speeches, activities, and directives from the pope and the Vatican was probably heavily influenced by his studies in Rome[3] and was accentuated by his three years as Archbishop of El Salvador (1977-1980). Romero's daily diary, copious recordings of his homilies, five pastoral letters, as well as his file of retreat notes and letters, paint a portrait of his being an erudite life. Few pastors have left behind such a recorded legacy.

According to several commentators,[4] Archbishop Romero did not write out his homilies. To keep informed on what was happening in the country, every Saturday he met with a legal team of young lawyers, where he heard abundant accounts of injustice and abuse inflicted on the people of El Salvador, especially the poor.[5] Afterwards, he routinely prepared his homilies into the early hours of Sunday. Aside from the scriptural readings, Romero used varied sources to illuminate the Word of God. "I study the Word of God that is to be read on Sunday; I look around at my people; I illuminate it with the word [of God] and synthesize it, in order to transmit it."[6] While preparing his homilies, he made frequent trips to the chapel. Finally, instead of writing out the homily, he prepared a note card with a few lines of his ideas. Although his Sunday homilies were usually more than an hour long, the people attending Mass inside the Cathedral and those listening to it on the radio were riveted by his every word.

During the three years of his episcopacy, Archbishop Romero gave approximately 196 homilies during the Sunday Mass that he celebrated in the Cathedral of San Salvador. He also delivered countless homilies as he traveled throughout the archdiocese; some were delivered for special liturgical feasts, while others were delivered at the funeral services for martyred priests and laity. If recorded versions of these exist, they have not been published. His Sunday homilies, however, were all recorded and, following his death, they were transcribed and published. The first transcribed homily was given on March 14, 1977, at the funeral Mass of Father Rutilio Grande; Romero's final homily was delivered on March 24, 1980, moments before he was assassinated.

Romero left behind a vast body of work that deserves serious treatment in its own right. But examples from some of his homilies and other works serve to highlight his charism as a gifted communicator of the Word of God.

Significantly, the published collection of Óscar Romero's homilies begins with the homily given at Rutilio Grande's funeral Mass in which he expressed his deep affection for the murdered priest:

> "If this were an ordinary funeral, I would speak here, my dear sisters and brothers, about the human and personal relationship that I shared with Father Rutilio Grande whom I considered a brother. At important moments in my life, he was very close to me and I will never forget his gestures of friendship. But this is not the time to speak about my personal feelings but to proclaim, in the presence of these bodies, a message for all of us who continue the pilgrimage of life."[7]

In fact, Romero mentioned Grande in his homilies on at least eight separate occasions.

In setting the theme of each Mass, as well as that of the homily, Romero embedded his words in the specific occasion for the celebration. Speaking as Archbishop, he used the teachings of the Church to relate the gospel message to the real situation of the day. At Grande's funeral, to give meaning to Rutilio Grande's life and death, Romero reflected upon Pope Paul VI's Apostolic Exhortation *Evangelii Nuntiandi*—Evangelization in the Modern World. The Archbishop posed the question: "What is the role of the Church in this univer-sal struggle for liberation from so much misery?"[8] His clear answer highlighted the Church's sacred obligation to raise its voice on behalf of the poor and the marginalized whose poverty reduced them to the most vulnerable and unprotected members of society.

Referring to Paul VI's message, Romero declared: "The Church can-not absent itself from this struggle for liberation, but its presence in this struggle must lift up and respect human dignity."[9] Liberation inspired by faith and based on the social doctrine of the Church had been Rutilio Grande's essential message. Both Romero and Grande insisted that the church's social doctrine was not to be confused with "the political doctrine that obstructs the world."[10] Everyone at the funeral who knew Grande was aware of the martyred priest's integ-rity and Christian commitment. Grande had always been careful to communicate to the people that he was preaching the Gospel and not espousing or promoting a political agenda. Romero also knew that Rutilio Grande loved God, and that love gave meaning to the martyred priest's life and ministry among the rural poor of El Salva-dor. Romero exhorted those gathered at Grande's funeral to commit to liberating the poor from oppression and to base their ministry on faith and on the love of God as Rutilio had so faithfully done in his lifetime.

In a Catholic country such as El Salvador, the murder of a priest was unthinkable. Grande's assassination shocked everyone including the new Archbishop. A scarce three weeks after Romero's installa-tion as Archbishop of El Salvador, he was made painfully aware that the country was experiencing "convulsive times" and that the Salva-doran people were at a crossroad in their history.[11] As Romero once confided to Jesuit Provincial César Jerez: "When I looked at Rutilio dead, I thought: if they killed him for doing what he did, it is my turn to walk along the same path…I changed, yes, but it is also that I returned to where I started."[12] Two months later, Romero had to deal with the violent death of another priest: Father Alfonso Navarro, the pastor of Resurrection Parish, and a young boy who was working with him, Luis Alfredo Torres, were assassinated in May 1977.

While the senseless murders of countless innocent people continued, at the funeral of Father Rafael Palacios on June 21, 1979, Archbishop Romero discovered another voice, which he evoked in the opening lines of his homily. He referred to "the voice of blood [that] is more eloquent than words." Regrettably that voice had become all too familiar to the listeners of his Sunday homilies. Romero acknowledged his task of "attempting to interpret the language of all this blood that has been shed in the mountains and the streets and the highways and the beaches of our nation."[13] But, he also saw his duty as shepherd to find in the bloodshed a message of comfort and hope. Increasingly Romero called upon the government to assume its responsibility for bringing the perpetrators of these criminal acts to justice. On behalf of the suffering people of El Salvador, he demanded of the government: "In the name of the citizens of this nation, I ask, I demand that this criminal action be investigated."[14] He had insisted on the same justice after the murder of Rutilio Grande, Manuel Solórzano, and the young boy, Nelson Rutilio Lemus.

In the subsequent months and years, Romero's homilies continued to address the increasing violence and repression. He consistently presented the events in the light of the Word of God and the documents of the Church such as those of the Second Vatican Council, Medellín, and Puebla. Contrary to his earlier rejection of the conclusions of Medellín, the beleaguered Archbishop had come to accept them as the authentic teaching of the Church. On March 11, 1979, the Second Sunday of Lent, Romero reminded the people of the significance of these church documents: "We must study this document [Puebla] and see the elements that are offered to us for the liberation, the beatification, the freedom and the dignity of the people of El Salvador. It would be very regretful if the same thing were to happen to the document of Puebla as occurred with the documents of Medellín, namely, because of preconceived ideas and many times because of ignorance, the pastoral guidelines of Medellín were not put into practice."[15] Archbishop Romero knew of what he spoke since he had once been among those who had rejected Medellín's teachings.

As the violence spiraled, Romero's word became that of the prophet whom God had sent to denounce injustice and announce justice. His words from the pulpit became the weekly "newspaper" for the people who were not always informed on what was happening throughout the country. He interpreted the people's successful fight to gain repartition of land, collective ownership of the mines, or resolution of labor conflict as signs of resurrection.[16] He publicly promulgated the lengthening list of the disappeared, tortured, abducted, and murdered victims. Romero's word was the voice of a shepherd who cared for and protected his flock.

Aside from homilies and other public presentations, during his three years as Archbishop, Romero wrote four pastoral letters; he had written an earlier one while he was Bishop of Santiago de María. During the turbulent years of his episcopal ministry, he spoke to the people as their pastor, instructing, directing, and consoling them.

Romero's first pastoral letter, "The Easter Church," was preached in the Parish of the Resurrection in the Colonia Miramonte neighborhood of San Salvador on Sunday, April 10, 1977, following the death of Rutilio Grande and companions. It served as Romero's formal introduction as the newly installed archbishop and marked the transition from the pastoral leadership of the retired Archbishop Chávez y González. It is believed that Romero wrote the letter on his trip to Rome, completing it on the connecting flights.

Focusing on the Easter themes, Romero invited the assembly to reflect upon Lent and the lived mystery of Good Friday that led to a flourishing of Easter life. While understanding the challenges and the risks of the difficult times in which they lived, the church was called to work for the salvation of humanity in Christ.[17] The Archbishop reiterated the fundamental insight of Vatican II: that the Church's mission was to serve the world. Amid the challenges that the Church faced, the Easter tone of the letter was filled with hopefulness. Once again Romero delineated the current reality, illuminating it with Scripture and Church documents to convey the Gospel message. In the midst of a maelstrom of pain and loss, Romero's words offered the people hope and consolation.

Guided by Scripture and documents of the Church such as those of the Second Vatican Council, Medellín, and Puebla, Romero's subsequent pastoral letters also addressed a complexity of urgent realities. On each occasion, Romero used the pulpit to teach and guide the people in confronting the unfolding events in El Salvador. His were always words of consolation and Christian hope.

While he wrote the first pastoral letter by himself, as time progressed, Romero widened his circle of input, drawing insight from theologians, lay ministers, pastoralists, and the common folk. An anecdote often shared by Monseñor Ricardo Urioste illustrates the Archbishop's willingness to consult and listen. The story relates that Romero was holding a consultative meeting with clergy and pastoral ministers to whom he listened carefully. During the break, the Archbishop left the conference room and approached a shabbily clad man who seemed to be asking for help. Urioste saw Romero bend over and appear to give the man money. Later, Urioste realized that Romero had, in fact, been asking the man his opinion on the same question that had been discussed in the meeting.[18] The once solitary and introverted Romero who had so often prayed to overcome his natural tendency to withdraw from people was undergoing the transformation for which he had so often asked of God.

Archbishop Romero also communicated with the people who wrote to him. From the years of his tenure as Archbishop of El Salvador, he left behind over 5,000 letters.[19] Although some of the correspondence was of an official nature, a significant number of letters were personal responses to letters received from ordinary men and women. His letters characteristically responded to the need expressed by the writer.

As a shepherd of the suffering church of El Salvador, Romero chose his words not only to console, instruct, and direct, but also to communicate hope and joy. At times, his was a word of encouragement in solidarity with the experiences of those who wrote to him. Two examples of his responses are offered.

> "God is speaking to us through the events, and through people. God speaks to us through Father Rutilio, through Father Navarro, through the campesinos etc. God speaks to us through peace, through the hope we feel even in the midst of much tribulation."[20]

> "Thanks to God who uses this humble servant to bring comfort to his most abandoned brothers [and sisters]. This is my mission as shepherd: to guide,

serve, be 'the voice of those who cannot speak,' denouncing sin and proclaiming the Kingdom of God and the liberating salvation that Jesus brings us."[21]

For Romero each concern or sentiment expressed by a letter writer merited a response. To a disheartened young man Romero wrote:

"Courage, boy. The great ideals in life are not achieved without effort and without work. You know that our Lord Jesus, being the Son of God, wished to share with man the world of work and effort. He goes ahead of us and invites us to follow."[22]

To adequately explore all the rich dimensions of Romero's spoken and written word would be a formidable task in its own right. At the same time, it is enlightening to consider some of the sources from which he drew inspiration and insight. Aside from the wisdom of the scripture and the church documents for which he always demonstrated a special love, he found inspiration in the people themselves to whom he was always available. As the situation in the country worsened, men and women rich and poor alike came to Archbishop Romero's office. Despite his other obligations, he received each visitor patiently and listened to their endless stories of suffering. Mothers wept for sons, daughters, or husbands who had disappeared and could not be located. Romero listened and comforted them in their loss, referring some of the cases to be investigated by his own legal advisers. Feedback from his legal team led to the archbishop's incorporating case accounts into his Sunday homilies. The experiences of human anguish and sorrow touched Romero deeply. He spent long hours in front of the Blessed Sacrament praying to God for wisdom.

Those who listened to him preach, including his own family members, recognized God's spirit inspiring Romero's words. His younger brother Gaspar testified that one morning he accompanied Romero to a small village where the people shared their simple meal with them. There were no chairs, and the Archbishop sat upon the floor joyfully eating the food that had been served without utensils. Gaspar remembers the happiness of his brother in the company of such good and humble people. Later that same afternoon, Gaspar accompanied Romero to an assembly of dignitaries. As Romero stood to speak, Gaspar recalled, it was as if a force greater than the man had taken over: "At that moment, my brother became transformed before my very eyes. It was as if he were another person."[23] Afterwards, when Gaspar asked his brother what had happened to him when he began speaking, Romero simply replied, "God who always accompanies me."[24] Many people experienced similar moments that revealed Archbishop Romero as a man deeply rooted in God. His word, shaped by the church that he loved and by the people that he listened to and loved, was essentially informed and inspired by the Spirit of God.

When hearing his homilies and other talks, those who had the privilege of hearing Romero described his manner as decisive and tranquil. He spoke with a warm and tender voice directly touching the hearts of his listeners.[25] Romero drew from multiple sources, the Scriptures, Church documents, theological works, newspaper clippings, personal notes, and many more. The fact that he spent each week trying to be aware of what was happening to the people humanized his talks and delivery. He recounted the incidents of injustices with which so many of his listeners could identify. Some claimed that Romero's homilies were popularly accessible because he referenced proverbs and sayings understandable to simple people. While this might be true in part, his talks reveal a highly educated individual with the clear ability to handle complex thoughts. Yet his humble and endearing manner won over the hearts of his listeners.

He had always been a gifted preacher, yet over the course of his episcopacy Romero's style changed. Sister Luz, Superior of La Divina Providencia where Romero lived, commented in an interview that Romero had been known for his beautiful preaching, for his spiritually inspiring word. But when he became archbishop the time had passed for a spiritualized preaching. Sister Luz recalled that those who had heard Romero preach before his tenure as prelate of San Salvador noted the difference in his style of preaching. He once said that he had become converted when he was named Archbishop. In those conflictive years, the situation in the country had changed drastically, and that is why Romero changed so completely.[26]

Romero once said: "With this people it is not difficult to be a good pastor."[27] The people had taught him how to be a good shepherd, as his homilies and talks attest. His word accompanied the suffering people of El Salvador in the most difficult times of the country's history. His word reached out not only to the people of El Salvador, but beyond its borders, proclaiming the message of justice, love, and compassion to all who would listen to his prophetic voice.

Rutilio Grande, S.J.

Unlike Archbishop Romero, Rutilio Grande did not leave an extensive collection of homilies or other written work. To date, it appears that there are only three written homilies that were subsequently published. But aside from those homilies, Rutilio left behind his personal files containing letters, fragments of homilies, and pastoral reflections. These pieces provide a glimpse into his ability to communicate in a style decidedly his own.

Those who knew Rutilio applauded his ability to communicate with the people of the countryside in language rooted in their rural existence. Despite his many years of education at home and abroad, Grande never lost the ability to speak in the style of the people from his small town of El Paisnal. He knew their popular expressions and their world of symbols and imagery. His words embodied the experience of peasant people who lived an earthy reality of hard work and meager resources. Always aware of the realities of the moment, he spoke in a timely manner relevant to a specific situation so that the Gospel came alive to deliver a prophetic message.[28] His homilies, letters, and pastoral reflections reveal his ability to adapt himself to his audience. Each of his sermons communicated something about the time and circumstances in which they were written and delivered.

Two of his three published homilies merit significant attention as they demonstrate the power of his word. His final homily, popularly known as the homily of Apopa, will be treated later.

Rutilio Grande's earliest published homily was delivered on the patronal feast of the Divine Savior of the World (*Divino Salvador del Mundo*) celebrated in El Salvador on the feast of the Transfiguration on August 6, 1970. At the time, social tensions revolved around issues of agrarian land reform, creating internal tensions within the Church of El Salvador. The Second Vatican Council's strong call for renewal both within the Church and in its relationship to the modern world stirred new challenges for the bishops in Latin America: "The joys and the hopes, the griefs and the anxieties of the men [and women] of this age, especially those who are poor or in any way afflicted, these are the joys and hopes, the griefs and anxieties of the followers of Christ" (GAUDIUM ET SPES §1). The Conference of Latin American Bishops in Medellín drew attention to the stark reality of the overwhelming poverty in their countries, and the urgency for a new evangelization. At a meeting in Guatemala in 1970, the Central American Bishops committed themselves to implement the conclusions of the Second Vatican Council and of the Council of Medellín.[29]

Despite these high aspirations, in reality, the bishops of El Salvador were not ready for such changes. During the First National Pastoral Week held in July 1970 in San Salvador, the bishops rejected the conclusions of the assembly so that their final document had no reference to the Second Vatican Council or Medellín. The bishops' revision of the Pastoral Week's conclusions distressed Rutilio Grande so profoundly that he felt obligated to publicly address the assembly, asking them to support the original results. His action, however, instead compromised Grande's good-standing with the bishops. Nevertheless, for the Feast of the Transfiguration on August 6, 1970, the bishops of San Salvador asked Grande to preach the homily in the Cathedral for the occasion.

The annual patronal celebration brought together political representatives, ecclesial hierarchy, clergy, religious, and lay men and women. To be invited to give the homily at this cultural and religious event was considered an honor. Although those who lived with Rutilio in the parish of Our Lord of Mercies in Aguilares were aware of how much it cost him to present himself in such a public setting, he accepted the invitation. With the usual distress and lack of confidence that accompanied him in such situations, Rutilio meticulously and conscientiously prepared the homily.

Aware of the controversial makeup of the congregation, he repeatedly reviewed whether what he had written was adequate and appropriate.[30] In such circumstances those closest to him observed Grande's fragility, a characteristic that he shared with Romero. Nevertheless, in the moment of delivering a homily or talk, Rutilio appeared to be transformed with confidence and oratorical brilliance. Salvador Carranza, S.J., a member of the ministerial team at Aguilares described the alteration: "He [Rutilio] always had problems. But not when he spoke in public. He was transformed and he would put himself in the place of those he was speaking to...and he had no doubts whatsoever. Prior to that he expressed many doubts... Such as 'should I say this or that?' This was very characteristic of him. Filled with doubt, he consulted a great deal."[31] Grande, however, had a great capacity to listen and when he finally came to celebrate the Eucharist his reflective understanding manifested itself. Carranza observed, "It was as if from the moment that he prayed 'in the name of the Father' Rutilio was a man without personal problems, as if the problems of the people became his problems."[32] Inspired by the Spirit, Grande projected a different persona, as on the day that he gave the homily for the patronal feast of the Divine Savior of the World.

Grande began the homily with the question: "Why are we here?" Suggesting specious answers to that challenging question, he formulated possible responses for those in attendance. "Am I here because this is a Mass that I would never miss or the religious ritual of the descent of the Divine Savior, on the afternoon of the 5th of August? That and the processions of Holy Week, I never miss them. Everything else I don't care about. I show up at church every once in a while; but I do not have clear ideas of what the reality of Christianity is all about nor about the gospel of Jesus as it relates to my own life, in regard to my country and the entire world. All the rest I don't worry about!"[33]

His question challenged the assembly to further explore what it meant to be a committed Christian in the real world and how that commitment related to an authentic celebration of the Eucharist. Intending the message for everyone gathered in the Cathedral, he pressed them to consider the heart of the question. Drawing a direct connection to the three words of the Salvadoran motto—God, Union, Liberty—he questioned whether these values had been actualized for the people in El Salvador. Rutilio intended the challenge for both the civic and ecclesial authorities present at the Mass.

He then turned their attention to the Scriptural role of Jesus as the prophet who entered fully into the lives of men and women of His times to proclaim the good news and denounce evil: Jesus as liberator of those who suffer. In denouncing the evil of His time, Christ died: a challenge for the Church and for all the baptized. In a Catholic country such as El Salvador, where everyone considered themselves baptized, Rutilio took and expanded that cultural religious norm. "We all confess ourselves as baptized, the sons [and daughters] of this nation. Our governors, the ministers of the state, the intellectuals and professionals, the employed, the military, tradespeople are baptized; all our campesinos are baptized, and before everything else all the priests, bishops, religious men and women are baptized."[34] He reminded the ecclesiastical and political authorities: "The Church in its sphere and the Government in what belongs to them, with mutual respect within their legitimate areas, must collaborate effectively, boldly, and urgently in order to promote 'just laws, that are honest and convenient,' as required by the sovereignty of the people in the first article of the constitution."[35]

In his conclusion, he urged the Church and the government "to transform the Salvadoran people living in the valleys, besides the beautiful lakes, along the Lempa River, at the edge of the flowering coffee plantations and channels, on the slopes of our mountains and volcanoes, in the villages and hamlets and the large growing urban concentrations and beside the large landholdings."[36] He exhorted that by addressing the real concerns of the people of El Salvador, the patronal feast of the Divine Savior of the World would become an authentic expression of faith, not an empty cultural gesture. Throughout this sermon, he wove together the actual reality of the people with the timely reality of a prophetic message. At the end of the sermon, Rutilio Grande received the two vastly different responses: a positive one from the President, and a critical one from the Salvadoran bishops. While President Fidel Sánchez congratulated him with the promised gift of a copy of the Constitutions of the Republic of El Salvador, the bishops frowned upon not only the content of the sermon but also Grande's specific references to their role and posture.

In this manner Grande's homilies resonated with the people. His first step along the path of ministerial commitment had been taken during his studies at Lumen Vitae as he realized the importance of full lay participation in the life of the church.[37] Salvador Carranza, Jesuit friend and team member, suggested that the August 6, 1970 homily for the Transfiguration, while powerful, focused primarily on the internal crisis in the church of El Salvador. From Carranza's perspective, Rutilio was yet to undergo another stage of conversion that evolved during his time at the Latin American Pastoral Institute (IPLA) in Bogotá in 1972. There Grande articulated his fundamental calling: to minister to the rural communities of El Salvador, or as he called it "*opción primaria y fundamental.*"[38]

Grande's primary and fundamental option to work with the rural poor shaped his homilies both for the Third Festival of the Corn (*Festival del Maíz*) and for the homily in Apopa in which he denounced Father Mario Bernal's kidnapping, torture, and expulsion from El Salvador.

By 1976, while Rutilio Grande's work in the parish of Aguilares was flourishing with the active participation of countless lay ministers, the economic and political tensions in the country were intensifying. The oligarchy-government-Church had formed an unhealthy institutional alliance[39] that branded dynamic pastoral activity as suspect and subversive.

In Aguilares, the formation implemented by the pastoral team was developing men and women committed to bring about gospel justice and equality for all. The campesinos began to look for solutions to eliminate the economic abuses that they suffered. The first and second celebrations of the Festival of the Corn (1974, 1975), reflected the campesinos' understanding of the value of community. Their insight facilitated the forming of groups to respond to the existing unjust economic and political situations. In a short time, many of the campesinos began to organize themselves politically to combat the injustices that oppressed them. Many of the organizers were the best ministerial leaders emerging from Aguilares. Despite Grande's cautions regarding the forces against them, the lay ministers saw their efforts as the imperative of their commitment as Christians.

In this context, the celebration of the Third Festival of Corn took place on August 15, 1976. The year before, El Salvador had hosted the Miss Universe Pageant. For the Eucharist of the Festival of Corn, Rutilio Grande grounded the theme of the Mass in the spirit of the Magnificat. Throughout the liturgy, he used the language, the colloquial expressions and images commonly used by the campesinos.

Referencing the beauty pageant that exalted women for their looks, and the attendant practices of buying votes to win and holding grand parties at the Sheraton hotel, he contrasted those pampered women with the campesina women who had been chosen to represent their rural communities at the festival because of the many ways that they *served* their communities. Theirs was the authentic beauty that the Salvadoran woman should aspire to celebrate. Anyone who lived in El Salvador recognized the clear cultural and societal allusions in the homily.

The campesinos at the Mass understood when Grande spoke about those who did not fear the LORD, who made the sign of the cross while they prayed, "In the name of coffee, in the name of coffee and in the name of coffee…!! In the name of the sugarcane, in the name of the sugarcane, and in the name of the sugarcane!"[40] The people at the Mass understood that Rutilio's reference was to the wealthy landowners who were their employers. Highlighting the dignity of campesino lives, at the Offertory Grande prayed: "We present to you, Lord, these offerings, the humble tortilla, hosts of our people; corn, the sweat of our people in their vital efforts from planting to harvesting…"[41] His homily, popular and timely, spoke to the tensions generated by politicians using political fraud to gain power and to the unrest among landowners who feared losing their economic advantages. His was the prophetic voice denouncing the injustices so prevalent in the world of the Salvadoran poor.

Aside from the three transcribed homilies preached by Grande, a few brief or partial examples of his homilies and popular reflections underscore the message of his preaching. One responded to the unprovoked removal of the street vendors from their stalls in the marketplace. On the last weekend in October, his homily opened with: "An incident occurred a few weeks ago. Before speaking about it, we have waited, reflected, consulted and prayed! But we can no longer remain silent. We must speak on behalf of God and justice."[42] Rutilio tells the community that effort was made privately to remedy the situation but that it was unsuccessful. The situation was known publicly. The vendors had been forcibly removed from their stalls by order of the office of the Municipality. Although Grande had investigated the situation to ascertain whether the people removed were guilty of any legal offense, he found none.

In his time as a professor, he had taught classes on the Constitution of El Salvador and knew it well. He exhorted the congregation, especially those who held positions of responsibility in the community, to know and follow the Constitution. He drew their attention to Article 24: "These are rights of citizens: to associate together to form political parties in accordance with the law and to join those already formed."[43] He reminded the people that the government had to adhere to the following obligation: "Therefore, you cannot pursue, harm and do damage to any citizen, by the mere fact of belonging to different political groups; that would go against the fundamental law of the Republic. It would be a crime against the fundamental rights of every citizen."[44] Consequently, Grande declared that the Municipality had no right to remove the street vendors from their stalls.

After having received the copy of the Constitution from President Fidel Sánchez Hernández in appreciation of his homily for the Feast of the Transfiguration in 1970, Grande's homilies often made vigorous references to the constitutional rights promised to the citizens of El Salvador. On one occasion, holding the Constitution aloft while delivering a passionate homily, he accidentally sent the Constitution flying down the center aisle of the church.[45] Despite referencing the Constitution in his homilies, Grande was very clear that his role as priest separated him from political partiality. During the homily on the occasion of the removal of the street vendors, he clarified: "I am conscious of what I do as a priest. I do not belong to any political faction because I belong to all the community. I am here to serve all the baptized of this parish, and all those who belong to different political groups, they are all baptized. They all have a right and duty…"[46] Lest there be any doubt of his intentions, Grande expanded his point: "We denounce this injustice as something that goes against the basic human rights, and naturally against the Gospel that as baptized persons we must comply with and live."[47]

All of Grande's homilies, correspondence, and other pastoral reflections were rooted in the concrete reality of the people, messages timely and prophetic. Another element contributing to the efficacy of his word was his ability to attend fully to what was being communicated. Working alongside him in the evangelization process of the Aguilares area, Sister Eva recalled Grande's incredible capacity to listen to people. On some occasions, the talk was effusive, but Rutilio inspired patience in her: "We must listen. We must listen to the people."[48] And because he paid attention to the people, he knew the reality of their lives, and from that knowledge understood how to engage them in the study of the Bible. While the people talked, he took notes to share later at team meetings. According to Sr. Eva, Grande was "a simple man, very sensible, very humble…He would tell the people: "We are going to study a grand chapter. We are going to think that this grand chapter is a hacienda—and that the verses are hectares or small pieces of land that you are responsible to work."[49] Grande formulated the model from his awareness that the people were accustomed to working small plots of land assigned to them. From the comparison, they could understand how to study the Bible section by section. His homey examples made the bible accessible to the campesinos. With his method of speaking from and to the people's lives, he formed many Delegates of the Word who were able to communicate the Bible to their communities.

Grande's approach and leadership in the formation of the laity in the parish of Aguilares was so effective that in 1974 alone there were 362 Delegates of the Word. From this group, many of whom were gifted communicators, emerged key leaders and organizers working for the rights of rural workers, e.g. Christian Federation of Salvadoran Peasants (FECCAS). For raising their voices in pursuit of justice for the campesino workers, a number of the rural leaders were killed by the military, a tragic aspect of the vortex of violence in El Salvador.[50]

Grande's rich correspondence contains evidence of the power of the word with which he was gifted. On Holy Thursday, April 9, 1974, he wrote to Benigno and Jesús Ángel, his Jesuit team in Aguilares, sharing his analysis of the developing situation in which the population of 11,000 campesinos of the area lived: "These are humble people of the surroundings of Aguilares and El Paisnal…From here large caravans go to work in the rich sugarcane fields, to earn a few miserable cents, while the owners of such properties place their large amounts of money in banks within and outside the country… All of these overlords (caciques) are agitated by the Gospel that demands brotherhood, equality and love among all men."[51] As Rutilio noted: "…all men possess the land. As clearly the Lord God says in the Bible."[52] Grande ended "his pastoral letter" by giving permission to read it to the people in Aguilares, if the team wished. He adds a series of pastoral reminders to insure that in his absence they not forget the care of either the children or the outlying communities.

Being a gifted communicator, Grande was invited to speak at various significant events such as the Feast of the Transfiguration or on the occasion of Archbishop Luis Chávez y González' golden anniversary of priesthood. Grande's friends, Jesuit brothers, archdiocesan clergy and religious and laity recognized his inspired and powerful ability to communicate with the public. One of the Jesuit seminarians remembered: "I was in Aguilares for my pastoral ministry assignment. I crossed in front of the Church in Aguilares, and heard Father Rutilio's passionate voice from inside. I don't remember the words he spoke, but I do recall the force of his words. It made me wonder, whether something malicious could happen to him."[53]

In touch with the world of the rural poor, Rutilio Grande spoke their language. Also comprehending his contemporary Salvadoran reality, he addressed the situations in the country, prophetically demanding the living out of the Gospel. From his uncanny ability to listen to the people, he gained the insight to speak about God in a world wrought with injustice for the marginalized. Although a fragile man physically and emotionally, when called to speak, Rutilio Grande drew his words from his trust both in the message and the faithfulness of God.

Archbishop Óscar Romero and Father Rutilio Grande each experienced human limitations in similar and yet individual ways. Despite sensing personal unworthiness, they both trusted fervently in

God's generous love. Confiding in that love, they used their skills and talents to the best of their abilities. In their relationship with God, Romero and Grande were men of deep prayer as they searched out God's will. Early on Grande discovered how important the presence of others contributed to his life and ministerial journey. For Romero, the journey unfolded more gradually, but he, too, was also shaped by the suffering of the Salvadoran people. The power of their words challenged the abuse of power and the mistreatment of the poor and marginalized. They relied on the Word of God and the documents of the Church to illuminate the current events of their times. Like the prophets of old empowered by the Spirit of God, both men raised their voices against injustice and announced the liberation of the oppressed.

ENDNOTES

1. Delgado, *Monseñor, Pro-manuscrito*. (BRP). 51-52.

2. Ibid., 48.

3. Ibid., 68.

4. These authors confirm in their writings that Archbishop Romero did not write out his homilies: James Brockman, Ricardo Urioste, Martin Maier.

5. Interview with Roberto Cuéllar, September 27, 2015.

6. Maier, *Monseñor Romero: Maestro de Espiritualidad*, 90.

7. Romero, "Dedicated Love," homily for the Funeral Mass of Fr. Rutilio Grande and companions, March 14, 1977. RTW, accessed 2015.

8. Ibid.

9. Ibid.

10. Ibid.

11. Ibid.

12. Maier, 104. Spanish citation: "*Y no fue poco lo que nos pasó al llegar al arzobispado, lo del padre Grande. Cuando yo lo miré a Rutilio muerto, pensé: si lo mataron por hacer lo que hacía, me toca a mí andar por su mismo camino… Cambié, sí, pero también es que volví de regreso.*"

13. Romero, "The Voice of Blood," homily at Fr. Rafael Palacios' funeral, June 21, 1979. RTW, accessed 2015.

14. Ibid.

15. Romero, Second Sunday of Lent: "Lent, the Transfiguration of God's People," March 11, 1979. RTW, accessed 2015.

16. Ibid.

17. Romero. "Pastoral Letter," in *Voice of the Voiceless: The Four Pastoral Letters and other Statements*, 61-62.

18. Ricardo Urioste lecture, "The Life and Legacy of Archbishop Romero," Santa Clara University, April 28, 2010.

19. Delgado, *Monseñor Romero: Sus Cartas personales*, 7.

20. Ibid., 15.

21. Ibid., 53.

22. Ibid., 158.

23. Interview with Gaspar Romero, March 9, 2010.

24. Spanish citation: *Dios que siempre me acompaña.*

25. Maier, *Maestro de espiritualidad*, 92.

26. Interview with Madre Luz (BRP) undated.

27. Spanish citation: *"Con este pueblo no cuesta ser buen pastor."*

28. Miguel Cavada Diez, *"Las homilías de Rutilio: Una voz que grita en el desierto,"* Salvador Carranza, Jon Sobrino and Miguel Cavada Diez, *XXV Aniversario de Rutilio Grande. Sus homilias*, 18.

29. See *XXV Aniversario de Rutilio Grande.* "Introducción a la homilía del 6 de agosto, en catedral," 38. No author cited for that section; most likely, author is Salvador Carranza, S.J.

30. Interview with Salvador Carranza, May 6, 2014.

31. Ibid.

32. Ibid.

33. *XXV Aniversario de Rutilio Grande*, 40.

34. Ibid., 46.

35. Grande, "Homilía en la solemnidad de la Transfiguración del Señor en catedral," in *XXV Aniversario*, 50.

36. Ibid., 50.

37. Carranza, *Romero-Rutilio Vidas Encontradas*, 30.

38. Ibid., 30.

39. Salvador Carranza, "Introducción a las homilías del Festival del maíz y de Apopa," *XXV Aniversario de Rutilio Grande. Sus Homilias*, 53. Author of this section is not cited but most likely it is Salvador Carranza.

40. Grande, "Homilía en el tercer festival del maíz," in *XXV Aniversario*, 63.

41. Ibid., 71. Spanish citation: *"Al presentarte, Señor estas ofrendas, la humilde tortilla, hostias de nuestro pueblo; el maíz, sudor de nuestra gente en su proceso vital desde la siembra hasta la cosecha..."*

42. APCSJ, An unpublished homily written by Rutilio Grande with the date Oct. 29, no year cited—assuming that the date refers to a draft of his weekend homily, it is likely to be 1976, or perhaps 1975. Spanish citation: *Un hecho ocurrido hace ya algunas semanas. Antes de hablar hemos esperado, reflexionado, consultado y orado! Pero ya no podemos callar. Debemos hablar en nombre de Dios y*

de la justicia.

43. *Constitución de la República de El Salvador*, Article 24, 1962 edition.

44. APCSJ, An unpublished homily written by Rutilio Grande with the date Oct. 29 (no year noted, see n. 42). Spanish citation: "*Por lo tanto, no se puede perseguir, perjudicar y hacer daño a ningún ciudadano, por el hecho solo, de pertenecer a diferentes agrupaciones políticas: Eso seria ir contra la ley fundamental y (_____) de la Republica. Seria un delito contra los derechos fundamentales de todo ciudadano.*" In the Spanish citation, the article of the Constitution that Grande may have been referring to is not included."

45. Interview with Octavio Cruz, May 12, 2014.

46. APCSJ, An unpublished homily written by Rutilio Grande with the date Oct. 29 (no year noted, see n. 42). Spanish citation: "*Soy consciente de lo que hago como Sacerdote. No pertenezco a ninguna facción política porque me debo a toda la comunidad. Estoy para servir a todos los bautizados de esta Parroquia, y todos los que, pertenecen a distintas Agrupaciones políticos, son todos bautizados. Todos tienen el derecho y deber de inscribirse en…*"

47. Ibid. Spanish citation: "*Denunciamos esa injusticia como algo que va contra los mas elementales derechos humanos, y naturalmente contra el Evangelio que como bautizados hemos de cumplir y vivir.*"

48. Interview with Eva del Carmen Menjivar, May 7, 2014.

49. Ibid.

50. "Introducción a las homilías del Festival del maíz y de Apopa," *XXV Aniversario*, 55.

51. Letter from Grande to Benigno and Jesús Ángel, April 9, 1974 (APCSJ).

52. Ibid.

53. Interview with Antonio Ocaña, July 1, 2014.

6

Detail, photograph of mural on the exterior of La Divina Providencia hospital, San Salvador, c. 2005, where Archbishop Óscar Romero was killed while celebrating Mass, March 24, 1980.

CHAPTER 6

CONFRONTING ADVERSITY, VIOLENCE, AND CONFLICT

Following U.S. President Nixon's 1974 impeachment, Gerald Ford assumed the presidency of the U.S., succeeded by Jimmy Carter in 1976. The U.S. recognized the fraudulent election of President Arturo Molina of El Salvador (1972-1977). As Communism was viewed as a threat to Latin American democracy, the U.S. funded the military in El Salvador.

Pope John Paul I was elected on August 26, 1978, and died thirty-three days later. In El Salvador, the Church, guided by the directives of the Second Vatican Council and Medellín, dedicated pastoral and ministerial activity to raising the consciousness of the faithful to the social and economic realities suffered in the Republic. These efforts drew the suspicion and antagonism of the dominant classes. In the U.S., Hispanic Catholics continued their work to become an integral part of the Church.

Confronting Adversity: Óscar Romero

Little in Archbishop Romero's life foreshadowed the explosive and ultimately heroic role that he would assume in the years of El Salvador's vortex of violence. His childhood, though shadowed by both the illness that engendered his shyness and also the early death of his father, gave him the love and spiritual guidance of a typical humble Catholic family.

His years of seminary and higher studies in a pre-Vatican II period developed many of his talents in spite of his first-hand experience of World War II and brief incarceration in Cuba. As an administrator and later as a bishop, he carried out his responsibilities with efficiency and faithfulness, all the time developing a deep sense of prayer and reliance on God's will.

Beyond the moral and spiritual faithfulness of his life and early ministry, Romero's greatest challenges occurred during his episcopal assignments. Although the situations that confronted him as a prelate were plentiful, the most critical moments occurred during his three years as Archbishop of San Salvador (1977-1980).

In June 1975, after Romero had been named Bishop of Santiago de María (October 1974) following more than two decades of administrative ministry in the seminary, he faced the first grave crisis in his jurisdiction. On the twenty-first of that month, local guardsmen killed several campesinos from the village of Las Calles and pillaged the hamlet. Hearing of the assault, Romero directly confronted the Guardsman commander to denounce the atrocity, but his protestations were given scant attention. He directed his outrage to President Arturo Armando Molina in a letter decrying the situation and its disregard for the lives of humble people. Several days later, Romero wrote a letter to his brother bishops giving an account of his protest of the Las Calles assault.

As Brockman pointed out in his definitive work on Romero, clearly at this moment in his life, Romero "still believed that the public authorities were not responsible for the crimes of their subordinates... and that it was better to work things out on the level of church authorities and civil authorities."[1] Romero continued to write and protest the unjust treatment of the people. Nevertheless, aside from condemning the cruel circumstances that afflicted the poor, he offered no concrete solutions for resolution. For his two years as bishop of Santiago de María, although Romero lacked the insight to strategically confront the oppression, he was expanding his awareness of the blatant disregard for the human rights of the poor in his diocese. He had yet to acquire the insight to strategically tackle the oppression.

However, almost immediately after Romero was installed as Archbishop of San Salvador on February 22, 1977, a mere three weeks later—March 12—he had to confront the shocking murders of Rutilio Grande and his two companions. The ruthlessness of the Grande assassinations impelled Romero to make several public statements condemning the brutal deaths. Speaking as Archbishop of San Salvador, he openly demanded that President Carlos Humberto Romero[2] immediately investigate the murders and bring the perpetuators to justice. The Archbishop vowed not to attend any governmental event until his demands were met. Romero's strong stand contrasted sharply with his earlier posture of trying to peacefully co-exist with the government.

The very night of Grande's death, the Archbishop ordered the excommunication of all those responsible for the murder of Grande, Solórzano and the sixteen year old Nelson Rutilio Lemus, and publicly promulgated the order through the radio station of YSAX.[3] The following day, March 13, an archdiocesan bulletin communicated the official ecclesial notice of the murders of the beloved pastor of Aguilares and two of his parishioners. The announcement noted that the Archbishop of El Salvador had "formally requested the President of the Republic to direct the competent authorities to conduct a thorough investigation to clarify such a horrific crime and punish the guilty."[4] The bulletin announced that a funeral mass for the three victims would be celebrated on the following day. Romero requested that the clergy, religious men and women, and the faithful "...pray for the disappeared and render a final homage to the martyred priest who gave his life for his sheep."[5]

On March 14, Archbishop Romero issued a statement contradicting the misleading account of the murders of Grande, Solórzano, and Lemus as reported by the newspapers of *El Diario de Hoy* and *La Prensa Gráfica*.[6] Romero emphasized that the three victims were killed because of "the intense pastoral, consciousness-raising, and prophetic work that the aforementioned pastor developed in all areas of the parish."[7] Romero also reiterated the fact that the President of the Republic had prior knowledge of the murders and had called the Archbishop; not vice-versa as the newspaper had reported.[8] As a culminating protest, Archbishop Romero announced that to demonstrate the solidarity of the baptized in the face of such a criminal act, subsequent to the burial Mass, only one single Sunday Mass would be celebrated in the Republic. This stance displeased Emanuele Gerada, the Apostolic Papal Nuncio of El Salvador as well as members of the wealthy families and others who felt that the Archbishop was depriving Christians of Sunday's Eucharist. In the following days, Romero issued more statements forcibly denouncing the disregard of life evidenced by the blatant murders of a priest and his two innocent companions. He reiterated his vow not to attend any government event until the President kept his promise of prosecuting the murderers. Right up to his own assassination, Archbishop Romero never attended another government event.

In choosing to publicly and staunchly confront adversity, violence and conflict, Romero stoked the displeasure of some of his own brother bishops. One of them, Pedro Arnoldo Aparicio, Bishop of San Vicente, wrote a letter to Emanuele Gerada expressing discontent with Romero. On July 3, 1977, the papal nuncio responded to Bishop Aparicio: "The same Cardinal Secretary of State begs me to address the matter with the same prudence and delicacy that the bishops used in expressing their reservations on the matter. Invite the Archbishop to review and moderate his own position on relations with the Government to encourage a search for an understanding to make the general situation of the country less difficult."[9] Although Romero, the Archbishop, vowed not to attend government events until the wrongs were righted, Bishops Alvarez and Barrera attended the inauguration of the newly-elected President Carlos Humberto Romero. During his three years as Archbishop of San Salvador, Óscar Romero faced constant opposition from his own brother bishops.

When Archbishop Romero experienced the rejection of the bishops, he tried to resolve it through genuine dialogue. In early July 1977, Romero received notice from Rome that Bishop Revelo, whom Romero had recommended to be the next auxiliary bishop of San Salvador, had informed the synod of bishops that rural catechists in El Salvador were influenced by Marxist teaching.[10] Romero cautioned his clergy in San Salvador to abstain from rushing to judgment on Revelo until the reports of the comments were verified.

Unfortunately, when the news from Rome confirmed Bishop Revelo's comments, Romero wrote directly to his nominee: "I think it a brotherly duty of candor to write you that your words in the synod of bishops, published here with the customary hubbub, have bewildered the priests and the people who are more understanding of our pastoral policy, and only have cheered those who defame the church with exactly the accusations and suspicions with which you have regrettably judged the catechetical expansion of the country."[11] Romero informed Revelo that it was best to delay his appointment as Auxiliary Bishop of San Salvador until matters were clarified. The conflict, however, was complicated by Revelo's defiant stance in the face of several ministerial requests made by the Archbishop. Romero tried his best to address the complex situation of Revelo. Even in the difficult circumstances, Romero's patience and desire to dialogue was admirable. In the ensuing years, nevertheless, Revelo taxed much of Romero's energies and diplomacy.

Motivated by Romero's posture in denouncing the increasing acts of violence, the Priest Senate of San Salvador wrote a lengthy letter to Jean-Marie Cardinal Villot, Rome's Papal Secretary of State. The clergy detailed the acts of violence afflicting the Archbishop and the Church of El Salvador: the assassination of Father Alfonso Navarro, the kidnapping and torture of Salvadoran clergy, the expulsion of international priests, the threats made against the archdiocesan centers of communications and of education, the military occupation of the town of Aguilares and imprisonment of some of its people. The Senate apprised Cardinal Villot that the Archbishop was responding to these violations by publicly condemning them, and by entreating the government not only to dialogue with the Church but also to respect its mission. The clergy assured Villot that Romero's actions were based on the faith and teachings of the Church; that in every instance, the Archbishop had courageously defended the human rights of those unjustly treated. They pointed out that Romero's actions had gained the support and admiration of different churches throughout the world. In conclusion the letter stated: "We believe [that the archbishop's actions] are based on the Gospel and the Magisterium of the Church and that it confirms our adherence to the Holy Father and the Magisterium from where it emanates."[12] From the priests' perspective, Romero dealt with the escalating violence with courage and as a faithful minister of the Gospel. With the government especially, he encouraged dialogue to bring about a better understanding of the Church's mission.

Archbishop Romero maintained regular correspondence with the papal representatives in Rome. He communicated the events in the country and the Church's rigorous effort to secure governmental protection for clergy, catechists, Catholics and, all Salvadorans.[13] In a letter to Cardinal Baggio, Romero gave a detailed report on the escalating cruelty suffered by the people of the Republic. He reassured Baggio of the Church's stance: "Our calls to non-violence and to justice and a Christian life based on the Gospel and the Magisterium of the Church continue in general to be attacked publicly and anonymously by those who feel affected."[14] Two months later, February 18, 1978, Romero received a response from Cardinal Villot who acknowledged the hard reality of the country, and who counseled him to seek "a common agreement with his brothers in the episcopacy."[15] Romero received Rome's responses with a mixed sense of comfort and challenge. His love for the Church and his desire to be a good pastor compelled him to continue to pursue dialogue.

The years during his episcopacy were marked by intense suffering for the people of El Salvador. With the level of cruelty inflicted on the citizenry, especially the poor, the small country of El Salvador teetered on the threshold of civil war. Under the guise of fighting communism, the United States provided military training and economic aid to the national military. Archbishop Romero wrote a letter to President Jimmy Carter asking that the United States stop sending military aid to the country. Asking for their support and approval, Romero read the letter to all Salvadorans during the broadcast of his Sunday homily of February 17, 1980. Thundering applause in the church signaled their overall approval.

Romero's plea to President Carter was clear, direct, and informed. In the face of the atrocities, Romero wrote Carter, "as a Salvadoran and as archbishop of the archdiocese of San Salvador, I have the obligation to see that faith and justice reign in my country."[16] In appealing to Carter's Christian beliefs and desires to defend human rights, Romero urged that the United States neither send military aid, nor interfere with the self-determination of the country and the peoples' right to organize themselves.[17]

On March 1, 1980, Secretary of State Cyrus Vance responded to Romero's letter on behalf of President Carter: "The Revolutionary Junta of Government has shown itself to be moderate and reformist…We believe the reform program of the Revolutionary Junta of Government offers the best prospect for peaceful change toward a more just society…"[18] In the end, $6 billion in military aid from the United States funded the twelve-year civil war in El Salvador that claimed the lives of 75,000 people. Nevertheless in fearlessly confronting the United States, Romero publicly defended the right of the people of El Salvador to determine their own history. Raising his voice, Romero spoke particularly on behalf of the poor and vulnerable.

On March 23, 1980, a few weeks after corresponding with President Carter, Archbishop Romero delivered his Sunday homily in the Cathedral for the fifth Sunday of Lent. As usual, the church was overflowing with people who came to celebrate the Eucharist and to hear Romero's homily. After acknowledging the presence of visitors from the United States who were in solidarity with the plight of the country, Romero declared for all listeners, those present and those joining the Mass by radio:

> "I know that many are scandalized at what I say and charge that it forsakes the preaching of the gospel to meddle in politics. I do not accept that accusation. No, I strive that we may not just have on paper and study in theory all that Vatican Council II and the meetings at Medellín and Puebla have tried to further in us, but that we may live it and interpret it in this conflict-ridden reality, preaching the gospel as it should be preached for our people. During the week, while I gather the people's cries and the sorrow stemming from so much crime, the ignominy of so much violence, I ask the Lord to give me the right words to console, to denounce, to call to repentance. Though I continue to be a voice that cries in the desert, I know that the Church is making the effort to fulfill its mission."[19]

Romero drew from the Scriptural readings for Lent for a homily later entitled "The Church in the Service of Personal, Community, and Transcendent Liberation." As was customary, Romero's homily was lengthy. After his reflection on the readings, he enumerated the ecclesial events that had occurred since the previous Sunday's Eucharist, including the celebration in Aguilares of the third anniversary of Rutilio Grande's death to which very few people attended, fearful of the ongoing repression in the area. He continued with a lengthy summary of the many violations of human rights that had occurred in that week's time. In the three years since Grande's death, the number of murdered, tortured, and disappeared Salvadorans had dramatically increased. Denouncing the injustices, informing the people of what was happening in the country, and publicly acknowledging their losses had become an integral part of the Archbishop's Sunday Eucharistic celebration.

In the conclusion of that Lenten address, Romero boldly directed his words to the enlisted men of the national military forces:

> "I would like to appeal in a special way to the army's enlisted men, and in particular to the ranks of the Guardia Nacional and the police—those in the barracks.
>
> Brothers: you are part of our own people. You kill your own campesino brothers and sisters. Superseding an order given by a man to kill, God's law must prevail: *Thou shalt not kill!* No soldier is obliged to obey an order against the law of God. No one has to fulfill an immoral law. It is time to take back your consciences and to obey your consciences rather than the order of sin. The Church, defender of the rights of God, of the law of God, of human dignity, of the person, cannot remain silent before such abominations. We want the government to understand seriously that reforms are worth nothing if they are stained with so much blood. In the name of God, and in the name of this suffering people, whose laments rise to heaven each day more tumultuous, I beg you, I beseech you, I order you in the name of God. Stop the repression!"[20]

The final words of Romero's homily were punctuated by the people's applauses. For others who listened to the homily, his words represented a challenge to the authority of the government and the military. The day before giving the homily, Romero had met with his consulting lawyers who provided him with the week's account of violence. As usual, he listened to their report ascertaining that all the facts were accurate before incorporating them into his homily.

On that particular Saturday, Romero had asked for their advice about directing his words to the Salvadoran army. After careful consideration, the lawyers felt that Romero's words could be misconstrued as the Church's usurping military authority and power. According to one account, Romero listened intently but did not comment.[21]

Sometime that evening as he prepared his address for Sunday, the Archbishop made the decision that in his homily the next morning, he would, indeed, address his brothers in the military. Romero understood the risk of speaking so bluntly; his life had already been threatened. The escalating intensity of ruthless repression underlined the extreme danger of publicly speaking out against the military regime. In the face of that increasing brutality towards hundreds of Salvadorans, Romero did not hold back.

As Romero took his stand against the oppression of the people of El Salvador, he grew in stature and courage. Madre Luz Isabel Cuevas who had known him for many years, shared that when Romero was made archbishop and first arrived to live on the grounds of the hospital of La Divina Providencia, his hands trembled and he had to follow a strict medical regimen. As the oppressive reality of the country worsened, however, Romero's trembling eased and his medicines decreased.[22]

Madre Luz further observed that the Archbishop refused to receive gifts offered by wealthy friends and admirers because "he did not want to sell himself for gifts received nor accept an elegant house because he wanted to be completely free, not to bind himself to anyone, in order to have the liberty to say or denounce what he felt he should do."[23]

Because he boldly denounced the sinful acts that were occurring in El Salvador, Romero lost many friends. As a private individual, he suffered from the rejection, but he responded: "I do not care. As a human being, I feel it. But I have to tell the truth. I am a pastor and I have to care for my sheep."[24]

Perspective

Despite his shy and introspective tendencies, over the course of time culminating in his years as Archbishop of El Salvador, Romero developed the character to confront harsh adversity. A man of fragile health and timid disposition, he drew strength from placing himself in God's presence and from embracing his responsibility as the "voice of the voiceless." Using his talent as a public speaker, he publicly and openly denounced the brutal crimes committed against the Salvadoran people. At every juncture, he encouraged dialogue to resolve the tensions and conflicts. Listening to the endless accounts of human deprivation and suffering, Archbishop Romero recognized in them the suffering face of the Crucified Jesus.

Confronting Adversity: Rutilio Grande

Like Óscar Romero, Rutilio Grande's spirituality began in his home and village. Unlike Romero, however, Rutilio's early life brought its significant share of adversity in the poverty and disintegration of his family who had to labor strenuously to provide basic necessities. Even his desire to prepare for the priesthood was almost thwarted by lack of financial resources until Bishop Chávez y González intervened. Again, in his time of training, difficulties of fragile psychological health and serious scruples assaulted him, but rather than deterring Grande, these early adversities honed his character.

From dealing with his challenges, especially those of health, Grande discovered that engaging with others contributed to his physical well-being. Instead of letting the geographical isolation that he experienced in Oña negatively affect his health, he initiated catechetical programs with the young people of the town. With his provincial and his friends he often shared the strategies that he devised to maintain his health. He prayed for God's help, yet he also put personal effort into preserving his well-being. In a letter written in Oña on April 9, 1956, to his Jesuit Vice-Provincial Miguel Elizondo, he shared the techniques that helped him to maintain his fragile nervous system: "I usually take ... some medicines that the doctor prescribed and that directly nourish the nervous system. With this and in taking advantage of vacation time all goes well."[25] Grande did not let his frailties excuse him from his responsibilities; in fact, he carefully guarded his medical condition from others, including his own family who were not aware of the fragility of his nervous system or of his diabetic condition. One of his Jesuit brothers remarked: "He knows how to internally carry 'his cross' and only when one lives with him or in personal conversation is a bit of his background revealed."[26]

The tenuous state of his health, however, contributed to a sense of insecurity when facing the public and caused him anguish in accepting difficult commitments.[27] Nevertheless, Grande confronted his fears with courage, working hard to fulfill his ministerial obligations. As his Jesuit friend Salvador Carranza wrote: "It was surprising how Rutilio drew strength from weakness. With much suffering, self-acceptance and unconditional faith in Jesus of Nazareth who all his life filled him with such enthusiasm…he managed to overcome his limitations and sicknesses. For those who personally knew him, it was amazing how Rutilio grew in difficult moments putting aside his limitations and proceeding with firmness and courage."[28] Overcoming adversity, external and internal, became an identifying trait in Rutilio's character.

In his priesthood and pastoral ministry, Grande faced many challenging moments, but drew upon his inner resources to respond to the demands of each situation. Imbued with the spirit of the Second Vatican Council, he wanted to change the traditional approach to priestly formation at the seminary of San José de la Montaña, but his vision was met with resistance from bishops, clergy, and even laity. Although their reaction distressed Grande, it did little to dissuade him from implementing his plans for renewing seminary formation, a daunting task in its own right. At times, Grande felt overwhelmed by the responsibility and even expressed to the Jesuit Provincial his wish to be released from the seminary obligations. "I am not in agreement with the way that the Seminary is being directed in aspects that are fundamental."[29] In an honest and direct five-page letter he detailed the multitude of difficulties that he encountered and the reasons why he felt that it was better for him to resign from the seminary.

Engaged in the life of the Archdiocese of San Salvador, he suffered keen disappointment when the conclusions of the National Pastoral

Week—held for the bishops, clergy and laity in San Salvador—were rejected. The edited document was not supported by the bishops, and changes that they made did not respect the will of the group. Grande himself found the bishops' changes unconscionable. But despite his discomfort in confronting the opposing voices, his letter to the Bishops Conference asked that they listen to the divergent views in the group. Even though he clearly explained the reasons for the request, the bishops upheld their assessment of the document.

Several months later, undeterred, Rutilio Grande accepted the request to address the issue at the monthly clergy meeting, on condition that he be allowed to speak openly. Respectfully but forcefully, he voiced his discontent with the bishops's position. He noted that what had occurred was partly due to the traditional priestly formation that bishops had received, which no longer responded to the needs of the modern world, a crisis that was occurring not only in the church of El Salvador but within the Universal Church. The contemporary world required a reconsideration of the role of the priests, a new call not only to explore creative pastoral approaches to current realities but also to conversion on a personal level. Despite the clergy's strong opposition to the way that the bishops had dealt with the proceedings of the National Pastoral Week, Grande encouraged dialogue as a way of resolving the conflict. In the end, he asked the clergy to focus more on the points in the bishops's modified document that they could agree upon rather than on what divided them.

While the clergy were persuaded by Grande's intervention, a former collaborator of the Salvadoran hierarchy, in a public newspaper criticized the internal tensions that the clergy had generated within the Church of El Salvador. Grande wrote several follow-up newspaper articles in defense of the clergy. In the face of painful conflict and adversity, Grande assumed a temperate yet courageous leadership position.[30]

Although the outcome of the proceedings of the National Pastoral Week seemed to be resolved, the bishops had not completely forgotten the criticism. A month later, Grande again drew the public displeasure of the bishops. Asked by the episcopal group to give the sermon on the Feast of the Transfiguration, patronal feast of El Salvador, his words challenged the bishops's reluctance to move ahead following the pastoral directives of the Second Vatican Council and Medellín. While the President of the Republic found Grande's homily moving, the bishops that were present felt publicly criticized. As a result, the Bishops Conference denied Grande's pending appointment as rector of the archdiocesan seminary.

The loss of his opportunity to exercise leadership in a renewed seminary formation disappointed and saddened Grande. Subsequently, he traveled to Bogotá to attend the Instituto Pastoral Latinoamericano (IPLA), a center that was actively promoting a renewed understanding of pastoral ministry in the spirit of the Second Vatican Council. During his time in the IPLA program, he stayed in correspondence with clergy, family and friends in El Salvador. When he anticipated his return at the end of his studies, he wrote conciliatory letters to several bishops in El Salvador, including Bishop Óscar Romero, in hopes of smoothing over any ill feelings that they might have in his regard. Even though Grande was honest in his dealings with the bishops, he also appreciated the art of diplomacy for the good of the Church.

Upon his return from IPLA, Grande was asked to accept the responsibility of overseeing the pastoral work of the Jesuit Central American Province. Although he loved the Society of Jesus and his vow of obedience, in honestly appraising his talents and disposition[31] Grande turned down the request; he did not feel adequately prepared for the task.

Grande assumed, then, the ministry in Aguilares cognizant of its many challenges. It required not only an investment of time and energy, but also the task of developing an innovative approach to rural ministry. Furthermore, the growing tension between the rural campesinos and the landowners was escalating. As the evangelization process in Aguilares advanced, the people acquired a sense of dignity and personal worth. They began to join the political organizations that were fighting for the rights of those who worked the land. Although Grande was always clear that his ministry was to announce the Gospel and not to become involved in politics, some of his best pastoral agents were joining political organizations and often assuming significant leadership roles. Despite the fact that his team in Aguilares was accused of promoting communist activity, Rutilio Grande never abandoned his parishioners. He continued to give them good counsel and to defend them when necessary. He never turned his back on those who needed him even when it drew criticism and dangerous attacks. His courage, however, did not relieve him of his distress and worry.

By 1976, the economic and social disintegration in the country created a dire situation of overall agitation. For the first time, El Salvador had a regional trade deficit and its general foreign trade diminished precipitously. Although the election for the new president was in process, the people had not forgotten the fraudulent election of President Molina in 1972.

Every day brought news of kidnappings, extortion, murders and expulsions from the country. Discontent grew among the citizenry and negative developments were facilely ascribed to an insidious threat of communist infiltration.[32] At the same time, ministerial work such as that in Aguilares under the pastoral leadership of Rutilio Grande, was monitored with growing suspicion. Catechists, delegates of the Word and active Christians became the targets of repression. The following year, the expulsion of foreign religious and priests escalated. At the end of January 1977, Father Mario Bernal, originally from Colombia in South America and now pastor in the town of Apopa, was kidnapped, tortured, and then expelled from El Salvador.

Father Bernal belonged to the Ecclesial Vicariate of Quezaltepeque of El Salvador; consequently, the Church in San Salvador took urgent action to publicly protest his mistreatment and expulsion.[33] The clergy and lay ministers working in that vicariate designated Rutilio Grande to be the spokesperson for the "manifestation of faith," as he called it, that was planned to denounce the abuse of church ministers.[34] Although Grande sincerely believed that Bishop Romero was the more appropriate choice as the symbol of the official church in the country, Grande reluctantly accepted the appointment. In the absence of Romero, Grande assumed the arduous task of preparing the public demonstration.

As usual, Grande left nothing to chance, painstakingly planning each detail. Beginning with an initiating procession through the streets of Apopa, the convocation culminated with Mass at the parish church of Santa Catarina where Father Bernal had ministered. Well-known as a gifted speaker, Grande was charged with delivering the homily. As was often the case, he anguished over his role and the efficacy of his contributions. His team member and Jesuit friend, Salvador Carranza, recalled that on the morning of the Apopa "manifestation of faith," Rutilio insistently reviewed all the details of the event with the Aguilares team. Fretting over the content of his homily, he asked them whether he had said enough; at moments such as these, all of his insecurities surfaced. At the same time when faced with monumental challenges, Rutilio Grande drew strength from a source greater than himself.

Grande's homily delivered in Apopa February 13, 1977, decried the numerous abuses that were being unleashed upon innocent people simply because they carried a Bible or spoke in the name of Jesus. Grande did not accept the rationale that Father Bernal was expelled from the country because he was a "foreigner." He refuted that pretext in the homily:

> "They tell me that he was a foreigner! Father Mario, a foreigner?! Certainly... and from Latin America. I wonder how in Latin America, discovered by Columbus where we are all kneaded together with coffee with milk as well as blood, we can be foreigners! Can we be foreigners anywhere?"[35]

However, the fundamental question he posed was: how does one live as a Christian in a world of such injustice? His homily courageously rebuked the few who held the economic wealth of the country in their hands.

> "It is not a matter that I say, 'I bought half of El Salvador with my money, therefore it is my right and there is no right to discuss!' It is a purchased right, because I have the right to buy half of El Salvador. It is a negation of God! There is no right that counts before those of the people! ... Therefore the material world is

125

for everyone, without borders. Therefore, a communal table with long tablecloths for everybody, like this
Eucharist. Each one with a seat at the table. And let
there be table, tablecloths, and food for everybody."[36]

Grande often referred to the communal table where everyone had a
place and a right to the banquet. For those assembled at Apopa, these
words were a familiar theme for Grande.

Grande forcefully proclaimed: "It is dangerous to be Christian in our
midst! It is dangerous to be truly Catholic! It is practically illegal to
be an authentic Christian here, in our country! Because out of necessity the world around us is rooted on an established disorder, in front
of which the mere proclamation of the Gospel becomes subversive.
That's the way it must be, it cannot be otherwise! We are chained by
disorder, not order!"[37] He suggested that in times like these, even if
Jesus of Nazareth might try to enter El Salvador, he would be condemned for his words and actions. Pushing the analogy further, he
asserted that the Bible itself would not be allowed in El Salvador because, from the perspective of those who oppressed the poor, every
word in the Bible was by its nature subversive.

A massive convocation of people participated in the Apopa "manifestation of faith." Most of them were inspired by and committed to
the pastoral efforts engendered by the Second Vatican Council and
Medellín. Not everyone present, however, was of that mind. Among
the crowd, surveillance agents were taping Grande's homily and ob-
serving all that was taking place.

Rutilio, however, was aware of the hostile element and of the potential danger it represented for him and the participants. In the homily,
he addressed the eavesdroppers: "Love that is conflictive requires of
the believers and of the body of the Church, a moral violence. I did
not say physical violence. Moral violence! I am saying it for the recorder, because I saw along the way recorders that do not belong to
the faithful who were listening to Father Mario; they belong to the
betrayers of the Word of God...."[38]

The potential for conflict was real. A third of the way through the
homily, the power was cut off leaving Grande without a micro-

phone.[39] But having anticipated disruptions, he had made provision to continue with a megaphone. There was no doubt that to the adherents of the status quo, the Apopa "manifestation of faith" represented a subversive and dangerous threat.

On February 22, 1977, nine days after the Apopa event, Óscar Romero was named Archbishop of San Salvador. With the country's uncertain situation, Romero's Episcopal ceremony was a simple private event. Grande attended the ceremony and afterwards with his usual diplomatic candor approached Romero: "You should have been there in Apopa, Monseñor. It would have been the perfect Episcopal installation and meaningful ecclesial presence; not holed up here, as several of the priests are forced to do."[40] Romero replied: "I understand, Father Tilo, but please understand my situation!"[41]

In his homily at Apopa, Grande underscored the importance of the Church's presence in the gathering.

> "At least to give a symbolic and official demonstration of protest from the Church, from our communities, from this part of the Church Archdiocese. He [Mario Bernal] was a priest in the local Church of San Salvador and specifically here, he was the pastor of Apopa, thus having a mission on behalf of the Church in this community."[42]

For Grande, it was important to express his displeasure at the absence of Romero at the Apopa ecclesial event. Grande and Romero's friendship dated back to the days when they both resided in the seminary of San José de la Montaña. But now that Romero occupied an ecclesial position of authority, Grande did not fail to extend the appropriate protocol of deference. Nevertheless, in this situation as in others, Grande faced difficult and uncomfortable situations with audacity.

Always alert to his delicate health and disposition, Rutilio Grande continuously prayed for God's grace to be at the service of others and to find the courage to face even the most difficult undertaking. Although many held him in high regard and affection, he was not a perfect man, but rather a good man aware of his limitations. He recognized his fragility and trusted in God as a child would in a father's love.

At the same time, he faced each moment of his life with hopeful tenacity. Throughout his life, confronting adversity, violence and conflict, he persevered to the end confident in God's love and compassion: a man of faith, a defender of the poor and oppressed.

ENDNOTES

1. Brockman, *Romero: A Life*, 54.

2. President Romero was not related to Oscar Romero.

3. *Boletín Informativo del Arzobispado*, March 12, 1977, No. 3 (BRP).

4. *Boletín Informativo del Arzobispado*, March 13, 1977, No. 4 (BRP). Spanish citation: "*ha pedido formalmente al Señor Presidente de la República, que las autoridades competentes lleven a cabo una investigación exhaustiva, para aclarar tan elevoso crimen y castigar a los culpables.*"

5. Ibid. Spanish citation: "*orar por los desaparecidos y rendir el último homenaje al sacerdote mártir que ha dado su vida por sus ovejas.*"

6. *Boletín Informativo del Arzobispado, Aclaración Arzobispal Sobre La Muerte del Padre Rutilio Grande, S.J. y Sus Acompañantes*, March 14, 1977, No. 5 (BRP). Spanish citation: "*se permite hacer la presente aclaración ante el pueblo salvadoreño, para borrar una imagen distorsionada y falsa del horrendo sacrilegio.*"

7. Ibid. Spanish citation: "*la intensa labor pastoral de tipo conscientizador y profético—que el referido párroco desarrollaba en todos los ámbitos de su Parroquia.*"

8. Ibid.

9. Letter from Emanuele Gerada, Apostolic Papal Nuncio to Bishop Aparicio, July 18, 1977 (BRP). Spanish citation: "*El mismo Sr. Cardenal Secretario de Estado me suplica de trabajar en el sentido de que los Obispos que han manifestado reservas en el asunto con prudencia y delicadeza, inviten al Señor Arzobispo a revisar y moderar su propia posición sobre las relaciones con el Gobierno, para favorecer la búsqueda de un entendimiento que haga menos difícil la situación general del País.*"

10. Brockman, *A Life*, 92.

11. Letter from Romero to Bishop Revelo, October 11, 1977 (BRP). Translation by James Brockman, *Romero: A Life*, 94.

12. Letter from Salvadoran Priest Senate to Cardinal Jean Villot, July 18, 1977

(BRP). Spanish citation: *"Creemos que ésta se basan en el Evangelio y en el Magisterio de la Iglesia y que confirman nuestra adhesión al Santo Padre y al Magisterio que de él emana."*

13. Letter from Archbishop Romero to Cardenal Baggio, December 12, 1977, (BRP). Spanish citation: *"Pediamos protección para los sacerdotes, catequistas, católicos y pueblo en general."*

14. Ibid. Spanish citation: *"Nuestras llamadas a lo no violencia y a una vida y justicia cristianas basadas en el Evangelio y en el magisterio de la Iglesia siguen siendo atacadas pública y anónimamente de ordinario, por quienes se sienten afectados."*

15. Letter from Cardinal Villot to Archbishop Romero, Feb. 18, 1978 (BRP). Spanish citation: *"...un común acuerdo con sus hermanos en el Episcopado"*

16. Archbishop Romero, "Letter to Carter," in *Voice of the Voiceless,*189.

17. See Archbishop Romero, "Letter to Carter," in *Voice of the Voiceless*, 189.

18. Cyrus Vance letter to Archbishop Romero, on www.csusmhistory.org, accessed 2015.

19. Romero Homily, Fifth Sunday of Lent, on RTW, 3; accessed 2015.

20. March 23, 1980 homily, RTW, 22; accessed 2015.

21. Interview with Roberto Cuéllar, member of legal advisors to Romero, Sept. 26, 2014.

22. Transcript of interview with Madre Luz, no date (BRP). Sometimes she is referred to as Madre or Sister Luz.

23. Ibid. Spanish citation: *"no quería venderse con regalos ni aceptar una casa elegante porque quería estar completamente libre, no atarse a nadie para poder tener así esa libertad de decir o denunciar él lo que tuviera que decir."*

24. Ibid. Spanish citation: *"No me importa. Como humano lo siento. Pero tengo que decir la verdad. Soy pastor y tengo que mirar por mis ovejas."*

25. Letter from Rutilio Grande to Vice-Provincial, Miguel Elizondo, S.J., April 9, 1956 (APCSJ). Spanish citation: *"Suelo tomar unas "ponzoñas" como dicen por aquí, o sea unas medicinas que me receto el medico y que son alimento directo del sistema nervioso. Me va bien con ellos. Con esto y con aprovechar bien las vacaciones ya va bien la cosa."*

26. APCSJ, fragment of personal comment of Jesuit brother.

27. Carranza, *Una Luz Grande Nos Brilló*, 11.

28. Ibid., 14. Spanish citation: *"Sorprendentemente, Rutilio obtuvo fuerzas de flaqueza. Con mucho sufrimiento, aceptación de si mismo y fe incondicional en ese Jesús de Nazaret que tanto le entusiasmo toda su vida, logro superar sus limitaciones y enfermedades.—Para quienes conocieron de cerca era casi increíble como Rutilio se crecía en los momentos difíciles dejando de lado sus limitaciones y procediendo con mucha firmeza y valentía."*

29. Letter from Rutilio Grande to Provincial, Nov. 30, 1969 (APCSJ).

30. See Salvador Carranza, *Una Luz Grande Nos Brilló*, 17-26 for a detailed account of this incident.

31. Ibid., 36.

32. Salvador Carranza, in Carranza et al, 51-52.

33. Ibid., 46. The following information provided by Father John Spain, M.M.: "At the time the parish of Aguilares "*El Señor de las Misericordias*" included the municipalities of Aguilares and El Paisnal and a part of the area south of the bridge to Chalatenango called Colima. Rutilio Grande, S.J. was the Dean of the Vicaría (Deanery) of Aguilares. It is now called the Vicaría de Rutilio Grande. The Vicaría included the parishes of Aguilares, Guazapa, Apopa, Nejapa, Quetzaltepeque, San Juan Opico and Tacachico." Email, November 17, 2015.

34. Ibid.

35. Apopa Sermon, translation by Irene Bubula-Phillips, Appendix.

36. Ibid.

37. Ibid.

38. Ibid.

39. See Apopa Sermon, Appendix.

40. Carranza, *Romero-Rutilio Vidas Encontradas*, 49. Spanish citation: "¡*Allí,en Apopa, debía haber estado Monseñor. Hubiera sido la mejor toma de posesión y presentación eclesial; no esta de ahora, aquí encuevado, como tienen que andar varios sacerdotes!*"

41. Ibid. Spanish citation: "¡*Entiendo, P. Tilo, pero comprenda mi situación!*"

42. Apopa Sermon, Appendix.

Detail of photograph depicting Archbishop Óscar Romero blessing the bodies of 16-year old Nelson Lemus, Father Rutilio Grande, and 72-year old Manuel Solórzano who died together en route from Aguilares to El Paisnal to continue a novena in celebration of the town's feast day on March 12, 1977.

CHAPTER 7

MARTYRDOM

In the world of the late 1970s, Soviet power was on the rise with interventions in the Third World and their invasion of Afghanistan. The Sandinista revolution in Nicaragua succeeded in overthrowing autocratic President Anastasio Somoza Debayle in July 1979. In the United States, President Jimmy Carter committed his presidency to the pursuit of human rights and new morality in American diplomacy.

In the 1977 elections of El Salvador, General Carlos Humberto Romero became President of the Republic amid allegations of political corruption and fraud. Massive violence marked the time between the presidential election and inauguration, followed by ongoing political protest and civil disturbance. President Romero was overthrown by a military coup in October 1979, and was succeeded by the provisional presidency of José Napoleon Duarte.

Following the death of Pope Paul VI in 1978, John Paul II, the first non-Italian pope in 400 years, strongly advocated for human rights. He used his influence to bring about political change, notably the fall of Communism in his native Poland and, consequently, the collapse of Soviet hegemony that had been strangling the people of Eastern Europe.

In El Salvador, the government intensified its attacks on the Church. The slogan 'Be a patriot: kill a priest' was smeared on the walls throughout the country, and two priests were murdered between March and May of 1977. Despite ongoing demands by Archbishop Romero, President Romero did not investigate the murder of Father Rutilio Grande and companions. In a letter to U.S. President Jimmy Carter, Archbishop Romero pleaded for an end of military aid to El Salvador. A few weeks later, on March 24, 1980, Archbishop Romero himself was assassinated. In the context of escalating violence and repression, economic and political factors prompted an unprecedented exodus of Salvadorans to the United States.

Rutilio Grande

In the days leading up to Grande's prophetic homily in Apopa, a series of events intensified the growing unrest in the country. The government in El Salvador was convinced that a number of priests were using the pulpit to incite the campesinos to secure better working conditions from the landowners. The formation of an organization known as FECCAS—UTC (Federación Cristiana de Campesinos Salvadoreños—Unión of Trabajadores de Campo) was gathering force. According to some of the Salvadoran bishops, Aguilares was one of FECCAS's strongholds. Aware that some of his parishioners were increasingly involved in FECCAS and other efforts, Rutilio Grande defended the rights of the campesinos to organize themselves according to the rights of citizens as conferred by the Constitution of El Salvador. At the same time, he clearly distinguished between the organizations and the autonomy of the parish. Each entity possessed a distinct identity and function. Grande was conscious, however, that he was still their pastoral leader and could not disassociate himself from those who were part of the Aguilares parish community.

As the tensions in Aguilares grew between the campesinos and the landowners, the rising water level of the Lempa River threatened the campesinos who lived along its banks. On December 5, 1976, afraid that the river would wipe out their humble shacks, the campesinos approached the landowners, Don Chico and Don Guayo Orellana. The people asked permission to relocate their living quarters out of the path of the cresting waters. As it was noon-time, the brothers, displeased by the request and by the interruption of their meal, faced the campesinos with firearms in hand. In the ensuing commotion, Don Chico accidentally shot and killed his brother Don Guayo. Although the campesinos were innocent of the violence, the following day the newspapers reported that the incident was instigated by rebel priests, such as those at Aguilares, who promoted violent confrontations. Reacting to the negative reporting, the Archdiocese convened to discuss the situation and took action to publish an article refuting the newspapers' claims.[1]

Within days of the Orellana brother's death, the appointment of Óscar Romero as the Archbishop of San Salvador was announced. The news dismayed the clergy who did not hold Romero in high regard.

The following month, January 1977, the wave of clergy expulsions from the country began. The brutal expulsion of Father Mario Bernal resulted in the "manifestation of faith" and Rutilio Grande's powerful homily in Apopa on February 13, just a week before the election of President Carlos Humberto Romero.[2] Nine days after the presidential election, Óscar Romero was installed as the Archbishop. With the heightened tensions across the Republic, Grande's homily in Apopa offended those who felt the church was meddling in politics.

Newly installed Archbishop Romero convoked a pastoral meeting on February 28 to discuss the growing presence of Protestantism in the country. The Archbishop asked Grande to speak on the topic. Given the more urgent issues that were besieging El Salvador, Grande considered the topic ill-chosen yet agreed to speak. A couple of days before the pastoral meeting, demonstrators gathered in Plaza Libertad to protest the fraudulent election of President Romero. As the number of protestors grew, the government sent troops to establish order. When orders to disperse were ignored, the troops fired upon the protestors, killing some while others fled to the nearby El Rosario Church.[3] As word of the bloody confrontation reached the pastoral meeting, Grande remarked: "My friends, here we are, up in the clouds, while in the Plaza Libertad, Salvadorans are killing each other."[4] The meeting was quickly suspended, but a few days later when it resumed, full attention turned to the intensifying attacks on the Church. The government arrested and deported three priests, a former priest, and two former Jesuit scholastics.[5] Some of those present at the pastoral meeting, recalled Rutilio Grande's forceful words condemning the government's action and exhorting the clergy to take a stand: "Those priests who would rather be hiding themselves away. Can they now descend to the valley?"[6]

The government's censure of foreign clergy directly impacted Grande. Several of his Jesuit team members in Aguilares were not Salvadorans. Keenly aware of their vulnerable situation and potential danger, Rutilio insisted that they not venture far from the parish and in some cases, he assumed their tasks. One of the team members, Salvador Carranza, had been assigned to El Paisnal as pastor. Carranza was a Spanish citizen, and his residency papers were about to expire.

As the town's patronal feast of St. Joseph approached, it was customary to anticipate it with the celebration of a novena. But Grande refused to let Carranza be involved in the preparation of the nine-day religious tradition. Rutilio himself, always fond of his hometown, welcomed the opportunity to creatively prepare the novena for St. Joseph. After the second day of the novena, Grande returned to the parish house in Aguilares and charmed his Jesuit brothers as he recounted how well the novena was progressing. Nevertheless, Carranza noticed that someone had slashed the driver's plastic rear window of the jeep. He carefully patched it, remarking to Rutilio that it looked like the shape of a cross. Aware of the threats against priests, Carranza beseeched him to be sure to park close to the church.[7]

The following day, the third day of the novena, Rutilio Grande left Aguilares for El Paisnal accompanied by Manuel Solórzano, a seventy-two-year-old delegate of the Word , and Nelson Rutilio Lemus, a sixteen-year-old boy. On route to El Paisnal, Grande spotted on the road three children who were hastily running toward home. He teased them about what their parents would say if they arrived late, and offered them a ride.

As Grande drove on the road that ran parallel to the sugar cane fields, shots rang out. Bullets pelted the jeep, some penetrating the repaired plastic rear window. Hit by the volley of bullets, Grande lost control of the vehicle, which overturned onto its side. The shooters hemmed in the jeep, allowing the three children to flee, who frantically scrambled over the wounded bodies and fled through the sugar cane, running at top speed. Young Rutilio Nelson was paralyzed by fear and died in the ambush. The assailants continued to shoot into both the front and the back of the jeep killing Rutilio Grande, Manuel Solórzano and Rutilio Nelson. Afterwards, one of the youngsters who had escaped recalled that in the final moments of life, Grande had said: "That God's will be done."[8] Father Rutilio Grande was forty-nine years old.

The news of the killings spread quickly. The afternoon Mass in Aguilares was about to begin when word reached the parish that something had happened to *Padre Tilo*, as he was affectionately called by the parishioners. In El Paisnal, the people were waiting for him to celebrate the Mass and the novena. Some people driving by the scene of the shooting attempted to communicate the information, but the telephone lines were not working. In San Salvador friends drove directly to the Archbishop's office, to the Jesuit residence, and to the radio station YSAX to communicate the news of the murders.

At first, confusion muddled the reports of what had happened. Many people recall that unforgettable night and how they first received notice of Father Rutilio's assassination. Sister Eva, his friend and co-worker, at Mass in a parish in Guazapa, remembered that a slip of paper was handed to Father Luis Ortega, the celebrant, with the words: "Father Grande has disappeared."[9] Father Ortega finished Mass quickly and immediately drove to Aguilares with Sister Eva. When they arrived, people from all the neighboring hamlets who heard the news with striking rapidity had gathered all around the parish area of The Lord of Mercies. Making their way through the throng, Father Ortega and Sister Eva finally were able to enter the church. Shocked, they found Father Grande's body laid out upon the table, the same table around which they had so often gathered for team meetings. Sister Eva recalled turning to Father Carranza and saying: "Please give me a towel because Father Rutilio's body is still dripping blood."[10] The blood quickly soaked the towel because his body had been pierced by so many bullets. "He was laid out in his usual clothes, with a black shirt, his priest collar, and his pants, now stained with blood…"[11] The sheer impact of thirteen bullets had almost dismembered his body.[12]

A few days earlier Father Rutilio Sánchez had escaped capture by government forces who had arrived at his parish to arrest him. Some commentators thought that Father Sánchez had been the intended target of the assassination and that Rutilio Grande had been confused for Rutilio Sánchez.[13] In an effort to discredit Grande, malicious rumors were invented to explain his murder. But Grande's indisputable reputation as a genuinely good man and pastor quickly dispelled such talk.[14]

Óscar Romero arrived in Aguilares around 11:30 that night. Sister Eva was still trying to clean the blood from Rutilio's body. The Archbishop stood in front of the body in a profound silence. After awhile he said, "If we do not convert now, then there will never be a time..."[15]

The death of Father Rutilio, a greatly loved pastor, was acutely painful to so many who loved and respected him. But the immense gathering of mourners surrounding him also filled the people with immense hope. Sister Eva looking around at the crowd of people remembered thinking, "Then he is not alone, we are not alone..."[16] The following day, even more people gathered having traveled from all over San Salvador, Aguilares, and its surrounding countryside.

That evening, Archbishop Romero with the Jesuit Provincial César Jerez and others celebrated a Mass over the bodies of Father Rutilio and his companions Manuel Solórzano and Rutilio Nelson.[17] A sorrowing Archbishop Chávez y González, who had mentored Grande from his early childhood and loved him as a son, concelebrated. He had wanted to be the main celebrant, but grief overcame him.

Around midnight, Romero gathered a group of clergy, religious men and women, and laity to discuss the next actions. They met in Father Rutilio's bedroom, and from that discussion emerged the plan to focus attention on Christian solidarity by celebrating only one Mass.

During that night, the Catholic radio station YSAX transmitted the account of the murders. Grande's pastoral colleagues, friends, and Jesuit brothers took turns broadcasting the news. Over the coming days, YSAX shared reflections on the events and offered recollections of the much beloved Padre Tilo.

At the time of the assassinations, Benigno Fernández, S.J., a member of the Aguilares pastoral team, was in Spain mourning the death of his mother. From a fellow Jesuit, he received a letter describing the events surrounding the death of his Jesuit brother and friend, Rutilio. For fear of government retaliation, the letter had not been signed. The unidentified Jesuit reported: "The bodies remained in the parish church of Aguilares all day Sunday, March 13, 1977. There was a continuous procession of people filing through in perfect order. On the morning of Monday the 14th, the bodies were moved for the funeral to the cathedral in three identical coffins. The cathedral was filled with a huge crowd of people, and more than one hundred priests concelebrated."[18]

Over 20,000 people attended the funeral Mass in the cathedral. From there the mourners began a procession, walking to the church in El Paisnal where the three victims were to be buried. Men carried the burial coffins on their shoulders. The number of the mourners was so great, however, that it was impossible to advance. Eventually, the three coffins were mounted on trucks to expedite the passage to Rutilio's hometown.[19] Upon arrival in El Paisnal, the bodies were laid to rest at the foot of the altar in the church: Rutilio Grande, S.J. buried in the center flanked on either side by Manuel Solórzano and Nelson Rutilio Lemus.

When the funeral services had concluded, and the people began to exit from the small town church, a group of guitarists played several songs that had been spontaneously composed to honor Father Grande, including *A Ballad for Padre Grande* composed by Jorge Palencia, which recounted the tragic events:

> "On the 12 of March of 1977
> they killed Padre Grande
> on his way to El Paisnal.
> Traveling with Padre Tilo
> the humble campesinos
> Manuel and Rutilio Lemus
> on the way to preach the gospel.
> Father Grande would say,
> those who have more
> should share the land of the wealthy
> for the poor have paid the cost."[20]

Benigno Fernández's unnamed correspondent wrote to him in Spain: "The following day there was a meeting of the clergy, more than 180 met with the Archbishop. A very long meeting, from 9:00 in the morning until 6:00 in the evening … [The clergy] strongly united with the Archbishop; the fruit of the sacrifice of Grande. There have been conflicts over the proposal to close schools (sign of solidarity as church), to have one mass on the 20th of March etc…But there has been unity with the Archbishop."[21]

Despite the opposition of the Papal Nuncio and others, Archbishop Romero was supported by the clergy of El Salvador and stood by his decision to celebrate only one Mass on the Sunday following Grande's funeral. As one of Grande's former seminarians said,

> "In the wake of Rutilio Grande, Archbishop Romero discovered the *pueblo*. And it included the priests. If we the clergy had not been organized to speak with the Archbishop to explain the situation, the Archbishop would have believed the government. He might have said: 'You are right. I do not want any more dead. I do not want any more murders. I will support the government.' But it is the organized *pueblo*, the people that made Archbishop Romero see that Father Grande died not only because he felt a commitment to the people, but because he was a good man. Through him, the Archbishop discovered that the campesinos had a right to organize. And that the organization is not meant to provoke the state, nor the dominant class. It is the ruling class itself that has these gaping jaws."[22]

Romero himself referred to the growing bonds of unity as the fruit of Grande's death. In the homily at Rutilio Grande's funeral mass, Romero said,

> "My dear priests, I am happy that among the fruits of this death that we mourn and of other difficult circumstances that we confront at this time, the clergy are united with their Bishop, and the faithful understand that there is one faith that leads us along paths that are quite distinct from other ideologies that are not of the Church—paths that offer an alternative to these errant ideologies: the cause of love."[23]

Although Father Grande died, his memory did not. Even years later, a former seminarian reflected:

> "Then what can I say about Father Grande? First of all, that even today when one speaks to many campesinos, they remember him as that kind and smiling man, who knew how to listen, who was atten-

tive to their needs, who evangelized with a word that was balanced, but always courageous and denouncing injustice."[24]

Perspective

A year after Rutilio Grande professed first vows with the Society of Jesus on September 4, 1947, his mentor and friend, Archbishop Chávez y González had sent him a letter encouraging his protégé to place himself under the protection of God and the Virgin Mary to maintain the treasure of his holy vocation. The archbishop wrote about the suffering of the persecuted country of Ecuador. In words that only later could be considered prophetic, the archbishop related to Grande: "If those who persecute knew that their HATRED fortifies the faith, perhaps they would not be so perverse...but the MARTYRS, who give so much Glory to God and so beautifully adorn the Holy Church, owes its crown to the wickedness of the persecutors."[25]

Indeed, the death of Rutilio Grande, S.J., the first martyred Salvadoran priest, brought about a resurgence and renewal of faith. He became the proto-martyr of a suffering country, a gift to the Church. As a native son, Padre Tilo was the sacrificial offering of a man who lived and died in solidarity with the struggles of the poor and marginalized. Soon after his death, other committed Christians would be added to the list of the martyrs of El Salvador, among them his former seminary students and countless campesinos.

His death fortified the faith of many, not only through the witness of his life and death, but in the compelling way that his influence extended through the lives of the young men that he had formed in the seminary and the campesinos to whom he had devoted his life. The memory of Rutilio Grande accompanied them through the dark and painful days of the civil war in El Salvador. As one of his former seminarians reflected:

> "...he had the capacity to make the [sacred] texts speak; to present them in such a way that the history of salvation that he spoke about was a history not only of the past, but it was the history that today is

also being realized. And, therefore, it was an invitation to discover the presence of God in our history. So that is what made us all wake up and transformed us, because it was not just to study things that God did in the past, but how to be attentive to that God who today is in our midst, and who speaks to us and sends us out on mission."[26]

Though Rutilio Grande lived and died in difficult times, it was also an era filled with the hope and promise of the resurrection. The power of God's word animated those whose lives Rutilio Grande had touched. He had mentored them to envision a Church committed to vivify the truths that were proclaimed in the documents of the Church and in the Word of God. Both "words" pressed for the response of a disciple of Christ in the difficult times suffered by the people of El Salvador. When he was a young Jesuit, Rutilio Grande had written in his retreat notes: "The Glory of God is in the unconditional surrender in love to God. This is fundamental. How it manifests itself is indifferent. Whether it be [acts] big and small. The greatest act that man can achieve is ridiculous compared to God. Only total surrender to Him, is, indeed, worthy of Him."[27] In the end, Grande fulfilled his youthful desire, unconditionally surrendering his life to God.

Óscar Romero

The assassination of Rutilio Grande and companions, occurring mere days after Romero's ecclesial installation in San Salvador, baptized in blood the tenure of the new Archbishop.[28] A swirling vortex of violence demanded Romero's immediate response. The murder of the deeply loved and respected Grande initiated a wave of vicious attacks throughout El Salvador.

The slogan 'Be a patriot: kill a priest' was smeared on the walls across the country.[29] Two months after Rutilio Grande's assassination, attacks against priests accelerated. Father Alfonso Navarro was murdered in the parish office of the Church of the Resurrection and with him a boy Luisito Torres. On May 12, 1977, Romero presided at the funeral mass of the young pastor who had been a former seminarian of Grande.

"Between February and July 1977, seven priests were refused entry to El Salvador; eight were expelled; two were killed; two tortured; one beaten; two imprisoned and four threatened with death."[30] A right-wing group known as 'White Warriors' ordered the Jesuits to leave the country or risk death. With the leadership of César Jerez, Jesuit Provincial, the members of the Society of Jesus refused to abandon the country and the people of El Salvador.

On the early dawn of May 19, 1977, the military of El Salvador initiated an offensive which they called "Operation Rutilio." Approximately two thousand government troops seized Aguilares. They cordoned off the town, cut the electricity, and occupied all the major buildings. With the possession of a photo of Rutilio Grande considered a subversive act, some parishioners hurriedly buried Bibles and any photos that they had of Father Tilo. Within an hour, the armed forces and police had searched every house.[31]

Father Carranza and his priest companions witnessed the destruction of the parish belongings and the soldiers' assault on the people of Aguilares. Carranza and other parish priests were jailed in a police station in San Salvador. From their cells, they heard the cries of men and women as they were jailed and beaten by the soldiers. Later the priests were taken to the border of Guatemala and expelled. Approximately, four hundred residents of Aguilares, mostly campesinos, were murdered.[32]

These acts of violence marked the beginning of Romero's tenure as Archbishop of San Salvador. Each destructive assault inflicted upon the people of El Salvador galvanized Romero's pastoral courage even as he struggled with his own fragile health.

Sister Luz recalled: "He was a sickly person. That is why the hand of God is apparent. He had always been frail and what drew one's attention was that despite the infirmities, during those three years of his archbishopric it looked like he always maintained his vitality."[33]

Denouncing one bloody violation after another, Romero's prophetic stance established a beacon of light and hope. Consequently, the wealthy class who initially supported Romero's investiture as archbishop denigrated the confrontational posture of the new Church leader. "This little boy turned out to be a naughty one."[34] Ironically their very condemnation brings to mind the biblical "little boy" David in battle against Goliath: Romero's prophetic word acted as the stone that each day defended the most vulnerable.

Early on in his tenure as archbishop, June 19, 1977, Romero said in his homily given at Aguilares:

> "I have the sad task of gathering up the bodies of those who have been abused, the victims of this persecution of the Church...Today I have come to gather up this church and convent that has been profaned, this tabernacle that has been destroyed and above all else to gather up this people that has been humiliated and unnecessarily sacrificed. Therefore as I finally come here—I have wanted to be with you from the beginning but I was not permitted to enter—I bring you the word that Jesus commands me to share with you: a word of solidarity, a word of encouragement, a word of orientation and finally, a word of conversion."[35]

For three years, Romero would continue to defend the lives of each abused and murdered victim. A growing number of his brother priests joined the list of the martyrs: Alfonso Navarro (May 12, 1977); Ernesto Barrera (November 28, 1978); Octavio Ortiz Luna (January 20, 1979); Rafael Palacios (June 20, 1979); and Alirio Napoleón Macias (August 4, 1979). Facing the violence, Romero searched out ways to protect the poor. He kept accounts of each precious life, and boldly wrote to U.S. President Carter asking him not to send funds to the military in El Salvador. Understanding more fully that the people had a right to organize and to assume responsibility for the future of the country, Romero did not hesitate to admonish Carter:

> "It would be unjust and deplorable for foreign powers to intervene and frustrate the Salvadoran people, to repress them and keep them from deciding autonomously the economic and political course that our nation should follow. It would be to violate a right that the Latin American bishops, meeting at Puebla,

recognized publicly..."[36]

Besides writing President Carter to denounce the interference of an outside power, Romero resolved to directly address the military forces in El Salvador. Appealing to the army's enlisted men in his homily of March 23, 1980, Romero demanded that they stop killing their own countrymen and women. "In the name of God, and in the name of this suffering people, whose laments rise to heaven each day more tumultuous, I beg you, I beseech you, I order you in the name of God. Stop the repression!"[37]

With the echo of his exhortation to the armed forces resounding in the cathedral, Romero concluded his Church commitments of that Sunday. Afterwards, Romero dined with the family of Salvador Barraza with whom he had been personal friends since his days in San Miguel, and who often drove Romero to his many pastoral responsibilities. On Sundays, the Archbishop frequently shared in the Barraza family's evening meal.

That Sunday evening of March 23, Barraza and the family noted a pronounced seriousness in Romero. In recent days, with the situation in El Salvador deteriorating, Romero's life had been threatened. Even his brother Gaspar had received two days earlier an anonymous note, "Tell your brother that his hours are counted…once kidnapped, nobody will know."[38] Although Gaspar shared the message with his brother, Óscar told him not to worry but to throw away the message. Likewise, when the Papal Nuncio of Costa Rica communicated knowledge of threats to Romero's life, Gaspar recalled that his brother's response was firm: "I will not leave, be transferred, or retire."[39] Nevertheless, the archbishop stopped having others travel with him; he feared that if something happened to him, that others would be harmed.

On the day after the homily addressing the armed forces, Romero worked in the morning and then went for a few hours to a gathering of priests at the seashore. Although he did not often have the opportunity, visits such as this one relaxed him. Later in the afternoon, Romero kept a doctor's appointment for a slight ear infection.

His friend and driver, Salvador Barraza, met Romero at the doctor's office. The archbishop had scheduled a memorial mass for the mother of a friend at six o'clock that Monday evening in the chapel of La Divina Providencia, but he asked Barraza to first take him to Santa Tecla so that he could meet his confessor, Father Azcue. They arrived in Santa Tecla in good time, and after his confession, the archbishop briefly enjoyed a cool drink that he was offered, but because he wanted to be back in time for the evening mass, they didn't delay at Santa Tecla.[40] Driving the archbishop directly to La Divina Providencia, Barraza dropped Romero off in time to celebrate the memorial mass for Doña Sarita Pinto, his friend Jorge Pinto's mother. On route, Barraza's last conversation with Romero concerned the building of a platform that the archbishop envisioned for the following week's Palm Sunday celebration.

A small group of family and friends of Doña Sara Meardi de Pinto and a hired photographer attended the mass. Celebrating the liturgy, Archbishop Romero delivered a short, ten-minute homily. Because he had so much to do that evening, he didn't want to be delayed. In the homily he offered a brief meditation on the gospel reading:

> "The hour has come for the Son of Man to be glorified…Unless the grain of wheat falls to the earth and dies, it remains only a grain. But if it dies, it bears much fruit. Those who love their own life will lose it; those who hate their own life in this world will keep it for life eternal. Whoever wants to serve me must follow me, so that my servant may be with me where I am." (JOHN 12:3-26)

Romero spoke of Doña Sarita's generous spirit and her concern for others in her community. Citing a passage from the Second Vatican Council, he reflected on the mystery of the world's transformation from deforming sinfulness to a new earth: "But we are taught that God is preparing a new dwelling place and a new earth where justice will abide, and whose blessedness will answer and surpass all of the longings for peace that spring up in the human heart."[41] He encouraged everyone to follow the example of Doña Sarita by doing what was possible to create a better world. Returning to the meaning of the Eucharist, he concluded:

"May this body immolated and this blood sacrificed for humans nourish us also, so that we may give our body and our blood to suffering and to pain—like Christ, not for self, but to bring about justice and peace for our people."[42]

When Romero returned to the altar to begin the offertory, he faced the congregation. At that moment a shot shattered the prayerful quiet of the chapel, and Romero crumpled behind the altar, bleeding profusely. Terrified and confused, most of the people fell to the floor for cover thinking that a bomb had exploded. Some of the sisters and congregants ran to the slumped body of Archbishop Romero. Turning him over, they found him gasping for air and covered in blood. Immediately, they placed him in a truck and rushed him to the Policlínica hospital. Although the doctors and nurses at the hospital tried desperately to save him, the Archbishop never regained consciousness and died soon after having arrived.

Romero's family was immediately notified and they began to arrive. Salvador Barraza who had driven him to La Divina Providencia in time for that 6:00 Mass, began to receive calls at home with the news that something had happened to the Archbishop. Finally, Sister Catalina called from La Divina Providencia and told Barraza that Romero had been killed. Barraza told his own family, then he and his wife Eugenia headed to the Policlínica. As he recalled, people were milling around the hospital, and it was almost impossible to get to the hospital ward. But because Barraza was often seen with the archbishop, he was accepted as a family member and allowed through and entered the hospital room where they had been attempting to treat Romero.

Barraza related: "That encounter with him was for me the cruelest of my life, the same for Eugenia, we embraced him. Each one that arrived cried, and offered us their condolences. They thought we were brothers because they often saw us together. Each moment was a cruel one, there was an exaggerated crowd gathered, all crying, touching him..."[43] Once Romero was pronounced dead, a decision was made to take him for an autopsy at a facility located in the centre of the city. But because the crowd made the removal of Romero's body impossible, the autopsy was performed in the hospital ward with only a few medical personnel and family members witnessing it.

147

The following day Romero's body was laid out in Sacred Heart basilica in San Salvador and a mass said there. The word of the Archbishop's death spread beyond the borders of El Salvador. In the three years of his archbishopric, Romero had touched the lives of countless people. His courageous stance against the senseless abuses and injustices afflicted on the poor of El Salvador exemplified true Christian commitment and pastoral leadership.

On Palm Sunday, March 30, 1980, the funeral mass for the slain prelate drew bishops, clergy, and lay people from many countries expressing their solidarity and admiration for Archbishop Romero. On the day of the funeral, the people accompanied Romero's casket in a thirty-minute procession from the Sacred Heart basilica to the cathedral of El Salvador del Mundo. The altar was placed outside directly in front of the main entrance of the cathedral and with more than 100,000 people attending, the Eucharist began with song. Despite the immense crowd in attendance, the funeral proceeded calmly.

After the gospel, the papal representative Cardinal Ernesto Corripio y Ahumada of Mexico City delivered the homily. As Archbishop John Quinn of San Francisco recounted later, the Cardinal was about

> "two-thirds through his prepared sermon when suddenly there was a sound of gunfire followed quickly by an explosion at the far right end of the square where the leftist groups had gathered. A sharpshooter had been sighted on top of one of the buildings in the square earlier...a second explosion threw the crowd into panic... Within seconds there were 5,000 to 6,000 people inside the cathedral. We were packed up against one another as in the old movies of slave ships. It was impossible to move and very difficult for the elderly and children to breath both because of the intense heat and because so many of them are of small stature."[44]

Hastily the body of Archbishop Romero was buried in a prepared tomb within the cathedral. For several hours the crowd of people sheltering inside did not know what was happening outside.[45] The plaza was covered in a sea of shoes discarded by the fleeing people.

Approximately forty people were trampled to death and many more were injured. The funeral mass for Romero remained unfinished.

In the context of violence and injustice Romero confronted the reality of his own death. Writing in his spiritual diary a few weeks earlier, Romero had considered the possibility of a brutal attack. During the retreat, Romero shared his fears for his life and the difficulty he had in accepting a violent death with his confessor who comforted him deeply. Romero wrote:

> "Father gave me encouragement telling me that my disposition should be to give my life for God, whatever the end of my life will be. With the grace of God I can live with the unknown circumstances. Jesus Christ assisted the martyrs and, if necessary, I will feel him very close to me when I give my last breath. But more important than the moment of death is to hand over all my life, to live for him."[46]

His blood spilled out upon the altar, Óscar Arnulfo Romero y Galdámez, had handed over his life to God. At that moment, Archbishop Romero of San Salvador joined the "Crucified Jesus" in redemptive self-giving for the "Crucified People" of El Salvador. He learned to live for them, and now he had died with them.

Perspective

A month before his death, Romero had received a Doctorate, *Honoris Causa*, at the Université catholique de Louvain in Belgium honoring his radical commitment to the poor of El Salvador. In his address, Romero said: "I am a shepherd who, with his people, has begun to learn a beautiful and difficult truth: our Christian faith requires that we submerge ourselves in this world."[47] Early in his episcopacy as Archbishop of San Salvador, he had to face the brutal murder of his friend, Rutilio Grande, the beating and deaths of priests and the systematic persecution of the people. Romero directed resources to care for the battered and terrified refugees; he opened the seminary of San José de la Montaña as a shelter and made sure that his priests gave the protection of refugees high priority.

The plight of the poor intensified Romero's comprehension of the desperate realities in his country. In an unprecedented move, Romero, the newly-installed archbishop, broke ranks with the conservative privileged class, personally engaging in the struggle to defend the poor and oppressed of El Salvador. In the end, Romero's fidelity to God in prayer, to the truth of the Gospel, and to the poor, positioned him to render the shepherd's full sacrifice of life for his flock.

Ultimately, the beauty of Romero's journey toward the fullness of Christian life is that he was an ordinary man who had to wrestle with his own frail humanity to live out his commitment as priest, bishop, and pastor. His human limitations marked his greatness.

In the city of San Salvador, a memorial wall has been erected giving testimony to the countless men and women who died during the ten years of civil war in El Salvador. The names of the crucified men and women of El Salvador are etched chronologically on this lengthy wall. Among the thousands of names listed, the name "Óscar Arnulfo Romero" is found under the year of 1980. He too is one among many of the victims of the bloody civil conflict. A retiring person by nature, even in death Romero's presence on the memorial wall eludes drama. Nothing extraordinary marks his place on this monument to national sacrifice and grief.

Óscar Arnulfo Romero, the child of Ciudad Barrios, had dedicated his episcopacy to the Sacred Heart of Jesus. After his death, his body was interred in the heart of his land in the Cathedral of San Salvador. On the grounds of the hospital of La Divina Providencia where he died, near the small house where he lived, his own heart was buried in the grotto by the feet of Mary. His journey completed, the prayer of this humble Christian man continues to rise to God on behalf of the poor and oppressed of El Salvador, indeed, of the world.

Óscar Romero and Rutilio Grande, born ten years apart, came from distinctly different social backgrounds. Their priestly formation carried them in separate directions and uniquely shaped each of them. Nevertheless, providentially their paths converged at the seminary of San José de la Montaña. At the time, Grande was one of the few, if not only, native Salvadorans on the faculty. Although Romero had studied at the seminary in San Miguel, he later traveled to Rome to continue his studies, eventually returning to the seminary of San José de la Montaña as a place of residence. Consequently, he was not personally acquainted with the clergy in El Salvador, and his overt criticism of the Jesuits who directed the seminary isolated him from potential friendships.

References indicate that Rutilio Grande looked out for Romero and eased the older man's interactions with the Jesuit community. From another perspective, perhaps Grande recognized the human frailty of Romero's personality and health because he dealt with his own "problems." However, in the course of my research, some of those I interviewed have discounted the close friendship between Romero and Grande that has become part of the "conversion" story.

It is difficult, now, to ascertain the actual degree of their fellowship. There is evidence, however, that Grande was consistently concerned for Romero and ready to help him. At a variety of junctures through the years, the younger priest turned to his own pastoral and ministerial colleagues soliciting their assistance for Romero. If the two men did not share a friendship of depth, their interactions suggest that there was a genuine mutual respect for each other. Neither of them would have imagined that they were both called to martyrdom.

A few weeks before Romero's death, José Calderón Salazar, a newspaper correspondent in Mexico, interviewed the Archbishop who disclosed his thoughts on death. The sentiment that Romero expressed might easily have been framed by Grande as well:

> "Martyrdom is a grace of God that I do not believe I deserve. But if God accepts the sacrifice of my life, let my blood be a seed of freedom and the sign that hope will soon be reality. Let my death, if it is accepted by God, be for my people's liberation and as a witness of hope in the future."[48]

Ultimately, the beauty in Romero's and Grande's lives is the fact that they were ordinary men subject to diverse and sometimes contradictory life forces, who consistently gave their best efforts to live out the Christian life. Their human limitations were the incentive for their complete trust in God. That was their greatness. Their martyrdom is memorable for the frail humanness that struggled toward it, and a comfort to the many women and men who labor in their efforts to make this world a more just one.

ENDNOTES

1. See Salvador Carranza, *Romero-Rutilio Vidas Encontradas*, 42-44.

2. President Romero was not related to Archbishop Romero.

3. See Brockman, *Romero: A Life*, 6.

4. Carranza, *Vidas Encontradas*, 49. Spanish citation: "*!Mis amigos! nosotros, aquí por las nubes, y allí, en el Parque Libertad, se están matando salvadoreños…!*"

5. Brockman, *A Life*, 6.

6. Carranza, *Vidas Encontradas*, 50. Spanish citation: "*Los sacerdotes que pasan encuevados. ¿Pueden ya bajar al valle…?*"

7. Interview with Salvador Carranza, S.J., May 6, 2014.

8. Spanish citation: "*Que sea lo que dios quiera.*"

9. Interview with Eva del Carmen Menjívar, May 7, 2014. Spanish citation: "*P. Grande desaparecido.*"

10. Ibid.

11. Ibid.

12. Carranza, *Vidas Encontradas*, 53.

13. Interview with Rutilio Sánchez, July 1, 2014.

14. Interview with John Spain, M.M., May 7, 2014.

15. Interview with Eva del Carmen Menjívar, May 6, 2014. Spanish citation: "*Si ahora no nos convertimos, no hay cuando.*"

16. Ibid. Spanish citation:"*Entonces no está solo, ni estamos solos, ¿verdad?*"

17. Ibid. See: Carranza, *Vidas Encontradas*, 55.

18. Letter from anonymous sender to Benigno Fernández, SJ, March 18, 1977 (APCSJ). Letter was not signed due to possible government repression. Spanish citation: "*Porque los cadáveres quedaron todo el domingo en Aguilares. Fue un desfile de gente continuamente y con orden perfecto. A la mañana del lunes 14 se trasladaron en tres cajas iguales para el funeral en catedrál. Un gentío enorme, la catedrál abarrotada de gente y concelebramos no sé cuantos sacerdotes, más de 100.*"

19. Interview with Rutilio Sánchez, July 1, 2014; Interview with John Spain, May

7, 2014.

20. Spanish citation: *"El día 12 de marzo del año 77' mataron al Padre Grande, iba camino a El Paisnal. Iba con el Padre Tilo los humildes campesiños Manuel y Rutilio Lemus a predicar el evangelio. El Padre Grande decía quien tenga mas que reparta la tierra de los ricos, es porque al pobre le cuesta."*

21. Letter from anonymous sender to Benigno Fernández, SJ, March 18, 1977 (APCSJ). Again the letter was not signed for fear of possible government repression.

22. Interview with Rutilio Sánchez, July 1, 2014.

23. Romero, Dedicated Love, Homily for the Funeral Mass of Father Rutilio Grande, March 14, 1977, RTW, accessed 2015.

24. Interview with Rutilio Sánchez, July 1, 2014. Spanish citation: *"Entonces, ¿qué quiero decirle del P. Grande? Primero, que todavía hoy al platicar con un montón de campesinos, lo recuerdan como a ese hombre bondadoso, sonriente, que sabia escuchar, que estaba atento a sus necesidades, que tenia una palabra evangélica equilibrada, pero siempre valiente y denunciante."*

25. Letter from Archbishop Chávez y González to Rutilio Grande, June 6, 1948 (APCSJ). Spanish citation: *"Si los perseguídadores supieran que su ODIO fortifica la fe, quizá no serian tan perversos... pero los MARTIRES, que tanta gloria dan a Dios y tan hermosamente adornan a la Santa Iglesia, debe su corona [a] las perversidad de los perseguidores."*

26. Interview with Octavio Cruz, May 12, 2014. Spanish citation: *"... él tenia la capacidad de hacer hablar los textos, de presentarlos de una manera a través de la cual esa historia de la salvación de la que él hablaba era una historia no solo del pasado, sino que es la historia que hoy también se va realizando. Y, por lo tanto, la invitación a descubrir al paso de Dios por nuestra historia. Entonces, eso es lo que nos hizo a todos despertar y nos transformó, porque no era solamente estudiar las cosas que Dios hizo en el pasado, sino cómo estar atentos a ese Dios [que] ahora también esta pasando, y que nos esta hablando y que nos esta enviando a la misión."*

27. Grande's hand-written retreat notes (APCSJ). Spanish citation: *"La gloria de Dios esta en la entrega incondicionada a Dios por amor. Esto lo fundamental. En que se manifiesta indiferente. Sean obras grandes y pequeñas. Lo mas grande q. el hombre pueda hacer ante Dios es ridículo. La entrega total a El esa si es digna de El."*

28. Interview with Roberto Cuéllar, Sept. 26, 2014. Spanish citation: *"bautizó con sangre el arzobispado de Romero"*

29. Michael Campbell-Johnston, "Be A Patriot: Kill a Priest," *The Way*, 48/4 (Oct. 2009) 14.

30. Robert Armstrong and Janet Shenk, *El Salvador the Face of Revolution*, South End Press, 1982, 92.

31. Carranza, *Vidas Encontradas*, 64.

32. See: Penny Lernoux, *Cry of the People*, Penguin Books, 1980, 62.

33. Transcription of interview with Sister Luz, no date. (BRP). Spanish citation: *"El era muy enfermo. Por eso también ahí se vio la mano de Dios. Siempre había sido delicado de salud y lo que llamaba la atención era que, a pesar de los achaques, durante esos tres años de su arzobispado se veía que siempre mantenía la vitalidad."*

34. Ibid. Spanish citation: *"Este muchachito nos salió malcriado."*

35. Romero, A Torch Raised On High, June 19, 1977, RTW, accessed 2015.

36. Romero, Letter to President Carter, in *Voice of the Voiceless: The Four Pastoral Letters and other Statements,* 189.

37. Romero, "The Church in the Service of Personal, Community and Transcendent Reality," March 23, 1980 homily. RTW, accessed 2015.

38. Interview with Gaspar Romero, March 9, 2010. Spanish citation: *"Dile a tu hermano que tiene las horas contadas... secuestrado, nadie va saber."*

39. Ibid.

40. Brockman, *A Life*, 243.

41. Last Homily of Archbishop Romero, in *Voice of the Voiceless*, 191-193.

42. Ibid., 191-193.

43. Salvador Barranza's handwritten account of the events of Romero's death and medical care. (BRP). Spanish citation: *"Aquel encuentro con El fue para mí el más cruel de mi vida, lo mismo para Eugenia, le abrazamos. Cada persona que llegaba lloraba, y nos daban el pésame. Pues téngase en cuenta que todas las gentes creían que éramos hermanos, pues siempre nos veían juntos. Era cruel cada momento, era una muchedumbre exagerada, todos lloraban, le tocaban..."*

44. Ibid. An account written by Archbishop John R. Quinn of San Francisco described the funeral event, April 7, 1980.

45. Brockman, *A Life*, 247.

46. CEE, 307-308. See also: Delgado, *Romero Biografia*, 190.

47. Erdozain, *Archbishop Romero: Martyr of Salvador*, 73.

48. Brockman, *A Life*, 248.

APPENDIX I

GRANDE: ON GOOD FRIDAY

Soledad is a Spanish transliteration, followed by an English translation, of a reflection by Padre Rutilio Grande, on the occasion of Good Friday.

Soledad

Se han ido todos, Madre, te han dejado sola.
Sola con el niño en los brazos como aquella noche de Belén!
Se han ido todos: Soldados y fariseos, mercaderes
E hijas de Jerusalén, apóstoles y sayones.

Toda la chusma, toda la pasta humana ha bajado a Jerusalén.
Con ellos nos hemos ido todos.
Para nosotros mismos, Viernes Santo es un momento…
después volvemos a lo mismo.

Arriba, en la cumbre, estás tú sola, Madre.
Sola con el Hijo dormido en tus brazos.
Todos los demás nos hemos vuelto al pueblo,
a eso que nosotros llamamos tan pomposamente:
Asuntos, negocios, quehaceres, obligaciones…

Tú sola, Madre, en el mundo con el quehacer,
la obligación de tener a Cristo muerto en tus brazos.
Nosotros tenemos otras cosas que hacer en la vida.
Tú sola, Madre, arriba con el quehacer de limpiar
con tu pañuelo, con tus manos, el rostro sucio,
ensangrentado de Cristo.

Mientras tanto, en Jerusalén, allá en la ciudad,
el bruto de Malco estará en alguna taberna, enseñando la oreja,
y diciendo que a él nadie le curó la oreja,
ni hay guapo que se la corte.
Y como Malco, muchos de nosotros,
fingiendo que Cristo no ha pasado por nuestra vida,

diciendo que nosotros somos tan brutos y tan plantados
como cualquiera…En una palabra: enseñando la oreja…

Tú, Madre, sola allá arriba
con tu Hijo en tus brazos. Mientras tanto,
en una fortaleza de Jerusalén, Pilato está diciendo a su mujer
que esté tranquila, que él ya se ha lavado las manos
doce veces en lo que va de día…Pilato es muy cuidadoso…
quiere estar a bien con todos:

A todos les ha dado algo: a los soldados
la coronación de Cristo; a su conciencia, agua y jabón;
al César, miedo y servilismo; a Caifás, la Sangre de Cristo;
a María de Nazareth permiso para desclavar y abrazar
el cuerpo muerto de Cristo; a Cristo mismo un letrón hermoso
que dice que es Rey de los Judíos.

Pilato ha atado todos los cabos,
ha hecho la componenda más asquerosa de la historia,
y ahora carraspea, se lava las manos por decimotercera vez,
y se dispone a tomar una buena cena con su mujer.

Como Pilato, un buen grupo de nosotros, que nos lavamos
las manos ante el sufrimiento de Dios y de los hombres,
y procuramos tranquilizar nuestras conciencias
haciendo estas clásicas componendas entre Dios y el diablo,
entre lo que quiere Dios y lo que nos da la gana a nosotros.

Los que sabemos subir, conservar un puesto a costa de todo…
Los que decimos que el negocio es el negocio y la vida es la vida…
Los que pretendiendo ser buenos cristianos,
preguntamos un día a Cristo ¿Qué es la verdad?
Pero luego nos escurrimos rápidamente para no oír la respuesta
Los que con tal de estar arriba, en el alto balcón,
jugamos lo mismo las cartas de Cristo y Barrabás…
y siempre nos queda en último término,
la salida de la jarra y de la palangana en los brazos.

Caifás esta noche cena con el suegro.
Están celebrando el triunfo y haciendo planes.

Otra vez a hacerse de oro y a abrir el negocio del templo.
A hacer del templo de Dios un mercado sacro,
y llenar el lugar sagrado de tenderetes para la venta de palomas y corderos,
para el cambio de monedas…otra vez el sucio cambalache:
la casa de Dios, cueva de ladrones,
y los dividendos para Anas y Caifás, sociedad limitada.
Se han vengado del Cristo que limpió el templo con el látigo.

Ellos eran fuertes, no en vano eran unos monopolistas
que tenían muchos resortes. ¡No ves, María?
Fíjate bien en el Cuerpo de tu Hijo:
ellos se han vengado de los latigazos con que tu Hijo les estropeó el negocio.
Ahí están en el cuerpo de tu Hijo,
los latigazos de Anas y de Caifás.

Ahí estás ahora sola, Madre,
sola con el Cuerpo arado por los latigazos
de la firma Anas, Caifás y compañía. ¡No sabías, Madre,
que en cuanto se nos toca el asunto del dinero y del negocio
ya no queremos saber nada?
Os quedáis solos: Cristo y tú. Al pie de la cruz.

Nos interesa un Cristo que multiplique panes y peces,
y dividendos e intereses y ventas e ingresos.
Nos interesa un Cristo que convierta el agua en vino
y las pesetas en duros y los duros en billetes de cien;
nos interesa un Cristo que llene nuestras redes de peces
y nuestros campos de cosechas
y nuestra cuentas corrientes de cifras positivas…

Pero, por favor, Madre, un Cristo
que emprenda a latigazos con nuestro comercio,
que descalabre las mesas de nuestros negocios,
que nos haga devolver lo robado como a saqueo…
un Cristo así, Madre, no nos interesa;
lo llevamos a la cruz, y luego te lo dejamos
A ti sola, Madre, muerto en los brazos.

Las hijas de Jerusalén lloraron un poco a la subida,
Pero ahora ya se han ido; es fácil que estén ahora riendo
por las plazas de Jerusalén.
Los hijos de Jerusalén lloran fácilmente un Viernes Santo,
pero luego olvidan fácilmente que Cristo ha muerto
y que tú estás sola con El en los brazos. Las hijas de Jerusalén,
que son buenas durante tres minutos, malas durante trecientos
y vulgares durante tres mil. Las hijas de Jerusalén,
que se cubren con el velo por la mañana, para que las vea Dios,
y se lo quitan por la tarde, para que las vean los hombres.

Los hijos de Jerusalén, que creen y parecen que son leño verde,
pero que Cristo dice que son leño seco. Los hijos de Jerusalén,
Madre, que han subido hasta la mitad del camino del Calvario,
solo hasta la mitad y luego han vuelto otra vez al pueblo,
dejándote a ti sola con Cristo…

Tampoco está Pedro, Madre; Pedro, que debía de estar aquí,
el primero de todos los hombres, contigo.
Pedro, el católico belicista,
el de las espadas y el de los mandobles…
El que después busca estar calientito al fuego,
mientras padece Cristo.

Y toda aquella multitud de curiosos se fue también ya a la ciudad…
Acudieron al gran drama de Viernes Santo como a un espectáculo
más…
como a una corrida de toros,
como a un partido de foot-ball…
Muchedumbre de Cristianos de nombre,
Católicos sin convicciones que esta misma tarde comenzaran su
vida rutinaria de siempre allá abajo en la ciudad, en el pueblo,
sumidos en su vida terrena y llamándose,
eso sí, Católicos de España.

Se han ido todos.
Todos los Cristianos pequeños que hemos dado media vuelta,
en cuanto nos hemos dado cuenta de que Cristo iba en serio hacia
la cruz.
Nos hemos ido a nuestros asuntos, a nuestros quehaceres.

GRANDE: ON GOOD FRIDAY

Quien sabe si también a nuestros rezos.
Un Cristo muerto era demasiado para nosotros
y te lo hemos dejado a ti sola.
La única que tiene fuerza
para sostener a un Dios muerto en tus brazos.

Y no nos juzgues demasiado mal por haberte dejado sola
con tu Cristo muerto.
Ya veras al tercer día,
cuando nos enteremos de que ha resucitado,
volveremos a creer en El los pobrecitos Cristianos de siempre.
Cuando la cosa esté menos fea,
ya verás cómo vamos volviendo todos:
Pedro, las hijas de Jerusalén…
y quien sabe si hasta la portera del pontífice
y el siervo de Malco.

Y tú, Madre, nos volverás a sonreír a todos, y harás
como si no te hubieras dado cuenta de que te hemos dejado sola
esta tarde de Viernes Santo.

Transcription by Ana María Pineda, R.S.M.
Santa Clara University

Solitude

Everybody is gone, Mother, and they left you all alone.
Alone with the child in your arms, like that night in Bethlehem.
Everybody is gone—Soldiers and Pharisees, merchants,
the daughters of Jerusalem, the apostles and those showing off.

All the crowds, all humanity is down in Jerusalem.
With them we all left.
For us, Good Friday is only a moment,
then we return to our same routine.

On the top, on the hill, you are all alone, Mother,
alone with your Son sleeping in your arms.
The rest of us have returned to town, to that which we call so pe-
dantically our routine, business, homework, obligations.

In this world of obligations, Mother, you are alone
while you have the dead Christ in your arms.
We have other things to do in this life.
But you're alone, Mother,
up there cleaning with your handkerchief, with your hands,
the bloodied and dirtied face of Christ.

In the meantime, in Jerusalem, in the city,
the brute of Malchus will be in some tavern, showing his ear,
and telling everyone nobody healed it,
and nobody would dare to cut it off.

And we're like Malchus,
pretending that Christ hasn't been in our lives,
showing to everyone we're as brute and arrogant as anyone else.
In a word—showing also our ear.
And you're alone, Mother,
on the summit with your Son in your arms.

In the meantime, in a fortress in Jerusalem,
Pilate is telling his wife to stay calm,
because he has washed his hands twelve times already.
Pilate is very careful, he wants to get along with everyone—
He gave the soldiers the coronation of Christ,

to his conscience, soap and water,
to Caesar, fear and deference;
to Caiphas, the Blood of Christ,
to Maria of Nazareth, permission to take down and embrace
the dead body of her Son;
to Christ himself a handsome inscription which reads
"this is the King of the Jews."

Pilate has found his closure,
negotiated the most nauseating deal in history,
and now he is coughing,
and washing his hands for the thirteenth time,
and he is ready for a good dinner with his wife.

Like Pilate, most of us, have washed our hands
when we see the suffering of God and human beings,
and we calm our conscience
while making deals with God and the devil,
doing what God wants and what we want.

Those of us who know how to climb the ladder of success
and like to be on top at all costs,
those of us who like to separate business from life,
those who pretend to be a good Christian,
but keep asking Christ "What is the truth?"
We leave swiftly so we don't really hear an answer.
We like to be on top occupying high positions,
playing our cards with both Christ and Barabbas,
but at the end we can take the easy way out
and wash our hands one more time.

Caiphas is having dinner tonight with his father-in-law.
They are celebrating the triumph and making plans.
A future of gold while already opening the business at the temple.
They are making the temple of God, a sacred market,
into a line of stands for the selling of lambs and pigeons,
a market exchange for currency.
A return to the corrupt market,
the house of God is now a cave of thieves,
and the profits are only for Annas and Caiphas.

This is their revenge against the Christ
who cleaned up the temple at the crack of the whip.

They are the strong men, and not in vain they have used their con-
nections with the powerful.
Can you see, Mother? Look carefully at the Body of your Son.
They found revenge from the whipping your Son administered to
spoil their business.
See there, on the body of your Son,
the whipping marks inflicted by Annas and Caiphas.

You are alone now, Mother, with the Body marked by the whips
signed by Annas, Caiphas and company. Did you know, Mother,
that when anybody questions our business, our money
we decide we don't want to get involved? The two of you
are better left alone then—You and Christ
at the foot of the cross. We are only interested
in a Christ that will multiply fish and bread,
provide profit and interest, and sales
and gains. We are interested in a Christ
that will convert the water into wine,
a dollar bill into a five, and the five into a hundred.
We want a Christ that will fill our nets with fish
and our fields with plenty, and our accounts with profit.

But, please, Mother, a Christ who cracks the whip
on our business, that destroys the stands at the market,
who forces us to give back what we stole so plainly,
a Christ like that, Mother, is not of interest to us.
We take him to the cross, and later we leave Him
to you alone, Mother, dead in your arms.

The daughters of Jerusalem cried a little up the hill
but they're now gone, and they are now easily laughing
in the streets of Jerusalem.
The daughters of Jerusalem cry easily on Good Friday,
but how soon they forget the dead Christ
and your loneliness with Him in your arms.
The daughters of Jerusalem are good for three minutes,
bad for three hundred and indifferent for three thousand.

The daughters of Jerusalem cover themselves with the veil
in the morning so God can see them
but in the evening the veil is gone, so men can look at them.

The people of Jerusalem, who believe they are fertile field
but whom Christ named infertile and dry.
The people of Jerusalem, Mother,
climbed up half the way to the Calvary,
and from there, they went back to the city,
leaving you all alone with Christ.

And how about Peter, Mother, who should be there and he isn't,
the first one who should have accompanied you.
Peter, the warrior, the one who loves the swords and the blows,
he was looking for warmth near the fire while Christ agonized.

The crowds of the curious are also gone to the city.
They saw the sacrifice of Good Friday like another spectacle,
like a bullfight, or a soccer match.
Crowds of Christians only in name,
Catholics without conviction—
This very afternoon they went back to their routine in the city,
embracing their materialist lives
and calling themselves true Catholics.

Everybody is gone.
All the petty Christians have returned as soon as we realized
Christ was seriously going to embrace the cross.
We have returned to our business, to our tasks,
perhaps even to our prayers.
A dead Christ is too much for us and we give Him to you alone:
The only one who is strong enough to hold a dead God in her arms.

Don't judge us too badly for leaving you alone with the dead Christ.
You will see on the third day, when we find out He is risen,
we will again believe in Him, us, poor Christians that we are.
When things are not that hard,
you will see how we all return to you:
Peter, the daughters of Jerusalem,
and perhaps even the gatekeeper's priest

and Malchus the servant.

And you, Mother, will smile upon us again,
you will pretend that you didn't notice,
that we left you all alone this very afternoon on Good Friday.

Translation by Juan Velasco
Associate Professor, English Department
Santa Clara University
February 2016

APPENDIX II

ROMERO: ON HIS FATHER'S DEATH

When Óscar Romero was a seventeen-year-old seminarian, his father died. Expressing his feelings, Óscar wrote this reflection on that occasion. A poetic English translation follows.

Lentamente va el sol a su ocaso.
La tarde languidece,
sus párpados cayendo tristemente robando
al día su esplendor…su alegría…su luz.

Qué triste esta la tarde ¿qué hay en oriente?
oscuridad, ¿tristeza, qué hay en poniente?
Hay luz, hay luz. Pero aquella luz en el parpadeo de una lágrima
amarga todo Dios mío todo habla de tristeza.

Pero dentro de mi pecho hay un atardecer más angustioso,
mis ojos perdidos tras las lejanas cercanías del oriente quieren hallar consuelo, pero el oriente, mi oriente inolvidable se ha convertido
para mí en ocaso, un ocaso enlutado.

Miro a oriente… y el oriente enmudece
bajo la triste sombra de una noche que ya empieza. Oriente mío
¿Qué me respondes?... ¡silencio profundo! Mi oriente llora.
Vendrá otro día, pero para mí, ese oriente, aún cuando se
baña de resplandores de amanecer, para mi seguirá llorando.

Mi papá ha muerto. Padre mío yo que cada tarde dirigía mi
mirada al lejano oriente, enviándote cariñoso mi recuerdo
lejano, te contemplaba en el corredor de mi
inolvidable casa, reclinado en la baranda azul, te contemplaba
dirigiendo tu mirada al ocaso donde estaba tu hijo.

Recuerdo que te oí una vez
"el poniente, los que ya declinamos al poniente"
"Ay, papá, ¿quién nos funde a mi mirada filial?

Mi madre, oh sí, mi mamá, pero y ¿tú, papá querido?,
ya no te contemplo vivo.
Tú, papá, se resiste a escribirlo mi mano, tú papá has....

Solo quedan recuerdos, recuerdos de la infancia, parafraseas
en el dormitorio, mientras mi entendimiento de niño grabando
el Padre Nuestro, el Ave María, El Credo, La Salve,
Los mandamientos, que tus labios de padre me van enseñando;
luego escuchar el cuento familiar bajo cuyas delicias
mis párpados de niño han caído y esta noche aún al rezar
con mis hermanitos.

Yo te veo una noche esperándonos de nuestro viaje a San Miguel
con mi mamá y que nos esperabas con un juguete a
cada uno, hecho con tus propias manos. Te recuerdo en los
viajes a la finca, trayéndonos pitos de carrizo. Y mi juventud
¿recuerdo tus esfuerzos por mi formación? Imposible
recorrer todos los recuerdos, pero aquí están muy vivos en
mi memoria y en mi corazón que te bendice.

Dios mío, apiádate de mi padre,
ten misericordia de él, perdónale,
Señor sus faltas, te ofrezco por él mis sufrimientos
y los meritos de tu gracia en mí.
Ten Señor, misericordia de mi papá
y que por fin goce de un rinconcito de tu Gloria.

R.I.P. Padre Mío, adiós.

      Spanish handwritten reflection by Óscar Romero
      Transcribed by Monsignor Ricardo Urioste
      San Salvador, El Salvador
      December 3, 2015

Reluctantly the sun descends leaving languishing hours
sad darkness falling
robbing the day of its splendor its joy
its light disappearing into a point of sadness.

Yet, God's light remains in luminous tears of sorrow
But my heart anguishes
light refusing to soften the distant edges
with consolation the horizon, my horizon,
shrouded in the doleful night that has begun

From my horizon
who listens, who answers only silence
I am dizzy with tears

Another day will come for me but this edge of being
though bathed in new light of dawn for me
continues to weep.

Death has claimed you, my Father
You who guided my vision to each far horizon
where my love follows you

I see you once again
on the doorstep of our home
as you lean against the blue railing
in the waning glow of the afternoon waiting for me, your son.

Your voice reminds me
"The sunset, all culminates in the sunset"

Oh, my Father,
who now embraces this son's love?

My mother, oh, yes,
I am comforted in my mother's love!
But you, my cherished father never to embrace you again!

Father, my hand resists writing of my desolation,
You my father.....!

I am left with only memories from childhood, sweet moments before sleeping:
the Our Father, the Hail Mary, the Creed, the Hail Holy Queen,
the Ten Commandments, a father's voice prompting a little son;
bedtime telling whose distant shadows wreathe the child
closing the night with prayers of brothers and sisters.

Memories, too, of lying awake in excitement all night
for the promised trip to San Miguel with mother,
and your greeting on our return with toy gifts
carved by your own hand;
visits to the farm delivering building needs.

Everything you did to shape my youthful life!
too many recollections to call back,
yet alive in my heart,
blessed by your love.

God our Father,
receive my father with understanding,
with mercy and forgiveness.

For my father, oh, Heavenly Father, I offer my sufferings,
the gifts of grace you have bestowed on me
that You may have Mercy on my beloved father
that he may glory in the splendor of your Presence.

Farewell, my Father, be in peace.

> Poetic Translation by Lourdes Thuesen
> December 4, 2015
> Lucerne, CA

APPENDIX III

GRANDE: *THE APOPA SERMON*

On February 13, 1977, the Salvadoran people protested the recent kidnapping and deportation of Father Mario Bernal. The people marched in procession to the Santa Catalina church in Apopa where Father Rutilio Grande celebrated the concluding mass and preached this sermon. This was but four weeks prior to his own murder.

Dear brothers and friends: The invitation has traveled through the valleys, the countryside and the villages where the voice of our dear Father Bernal would resonate through the waves with his classic "All right?!" when he handled the Bible. I would like to tell you, then, this invitation was sent to the Christian communities in the parishes of Guazapa, Nejapa, Quezaltepeque, Opico, Ciudad Arce, Aguilares and Tacachico. Our Vicar said that they are the parishes north of La Libertad and San Salvador.

We held an emergency meeting, the priests together with the Christian faithful of our parish, and we agreed precisely to have this manifestation of faith. We clearly announced that we would meet at the gas station and from there we would march in an orderly and organized fashion all together, united, in solidarity, confessing our faith, and then we would finish with the Eucharist that is the greatest commitment and the symbol of what Father Mario Bernal preached and defended.

It's the symbol of a communal table,
with a seat for each one and long tablecloths for all.
It is the symbol of Creation, for which Redemption is needed.
It is already being sealed by martyrdom!

Introduction: the Church as service institution

Now, my dear friends and brothers, allow me to tell you this, after hearing the Good News and the Word of God in this reading from the Gospel. We are part of a church formed by laypeople—you are

169

the majority of God's people. And if we have climbed here on these stands, the only purpose for our ministry is to serve you. The word "minister" comes from "to minister," meaning to serve God's people. From the Pope to the Bishops to the last country priest, we are servants in the community that is God's people. The Church is certainly an institution. This is required for a series of logical reasons, provided that this institution faithfully embody the values of the gospel, in order to make the world more dynamic, making it ferment, like bread dough ferments with yeast, reactivating it.

The Church must not be a museum of dead traditions, of gravediggers. It extends through all nations, languages, races and a diversity of cultures in the world, in the actual realities of the peoples. We are not talking in Japan, but rather here in our country, and the Word of God must become incarnate in this country.

We are aware of our fragility, our sins, and betrayals on the long road of history. We are a corporation of humans, the Church is human, from laypeople to Church leaders, priests and bishops and popes. We have confessed our faults and the constant need for individual and group conversion within the Church. The Pope has set an example of this on many occasions. Arriving in Jerusalem he threw himself on the dirty ground and recognized his fault and the fault of the Church for many of the sins of the world. The Pope is a weak man and a sinner, we are weak and sinners. This was said in one of the readings at the first stop: Where will we go to announce what the Lord gives to us, if we are poor?!

We are not here, in Apopa, this morning, a large number of parish communities are represented here, like a split sect of the Church, neither from the local Church, nor from the Universal Church. We feel part of this Church that we love, and we want to see it always renewed by the power of the Holy Spirit, in the midst of its weaknesses, that are indeed there; in the midst of evil, in the midst of all the problems of the world. We love it, not only for what the Church should be, but also for what it is already, in need of constant conversion.

First Part: Equality of God's Children

My dear friends, before we get to the central topic of this Eucharist, allow me to elaborate in this reflection. The Gospel that we have just heard is clear and clean like water coming down a mountain. Only the blind cannot understand it! Jesus was a walking pilgrim among the people. He would travel through towns and villages. He would preach the Good News of God's Kingdom in every hamlet, in every place, at every crossroad. And what are the guidelines of that Kingdom, of his first message? They are well defined, they are very clear, they are very precise. It takes evil; it takes blindness not to understand them!

We, all human beings, have one common Father. Then we are all children of this Father, although we were born from the different mothers here on earth. Then all human beings are clearly brothers and sisters. All equal one to the other! But Cain is an abortion in God's Plan, and groups of Cains do exist. He is also a negation of God's Kingdom. Here in our country there are groups of Cains, and what is worse, they invoke God.

God, the Lord, in his plan for us, gave us a material world. Like this material mass, with the material bread and the material chalice that we will raise in honor of Christ, the Lord. A material world for everybody without borders. This is how Genesis describes it. It is not a matter that I say, "I bought half of El Salvador with my money, therefore it is my right and there is no right to discuss!" It is a purchased right, because I have the right to buy half of El Salvador. It is a negation of God! There is no right that counts before those of the people! Therefore the material world is for everyone, without borders. Therefore, a communal table with long tablecloths for everybody, like this Eucharist. Each one with a seat at the table. And let there be table, tablecloths and food for everybody. There is a reason Christ chose to exemplify the Kingdom as a supper. He talked a lot of a banquet, of a supper. And he celebrated it the eve of his final commitment. He, at the age of thirty-three, celebrated a farewell supper with his closest friends. And he said that that it was the great memorial of Redemption. A table shared in brotherhood, with a seat and a place for everyone.

Love, the Code of the Kingdom! It is the only key word that sums all the ethical codes of humankind; it elevates them and unites them into Jesus. It is the love of a shared brotherhood that breaks down and destroys all types of barriers, prejudice, and must overcome hatred itself. We are not here because we hate! We even love those Cains. Those are our enemies—clearly they don't understand this! Christians do not have enemies. They are our brothers Cains. We do not hate anybody. Love that is conflictive and that requires of the believers and of the body of the Church, a moral violence. I did not say physical violence. Moral violence! I am saying it for the recorder, because I saw along the way recorders that do not belong to the faithful who were listening to Father Mario; they belong to the betrayers of the Word of God. [Applause interruption] Please let's not applaud, this way we are not going to finish!

Love that is conflictive and that requires of the believers, and of the body of the Church, moral violence. I already said that we were not to come here with machetes. This is not our violence. The violence is in the Word of God that forces us and forces society, that unites us and gathers us together even when we are beaten. Therefore, the code can be summed in one word, LOVE: against hatred, against sin, against injustice, against human domination against the destruction of brotherhood.

The message of Jesus is not just to announce the Kingdom and denounce its antithesis. The gospel we have heard says word for word: "Seeing the people, He felt compassion for them, because they were distressed and dispirited like sheep without a shepherd." Besides bestowing people with his prophetic words "nobody has spoken like this man" he also puts at their disposal all his capabilities, his walks, his qualities and talents, his power as a miracle worker: "He healed every kind of disease and illness," said the reader of the Word of God.

This means that the Lord was not indifferent to human pain. Not at all! The Lord gave bread and multiplied bread. This shows how his words became actions, as it is understood in the Bible: words are actions. He himself is the Word of the Father, he is action. He never stopped along the way.

My friends: As the Ecclesial Body, the Church and each one of us who forms it are prophets—as the brothers who preached the truth along our procession said. As an ecclesial body we continue Jesus' mission. This body that is the Church and that encompasses entire communities, has the mission, that is the task, to announce and facilitate a favorable environment for God's Kingdom here, in this world. It is necessary to embody the values of the Kingdom in the realities of our country to change it effectively, like yeast changes the dough.

One of our brothers already described very clearly the mission at the beginning of the procession. It is demanding: "I am sending you". And it is telling that to the Church and also to each one of us: "Go and tell the people!". And the people are made up of different groups. And the prophet must be confronted with the Word of God in his hand. The word of God is a pillar. It is the divine reality. God's message is like a thermometer and a pendulum to measure human realities, like a demand of the realities that involve all the different groups in our country: the Cains and those who are like Abel, that is, martyred, those who are being enslaved. Then, we all have a prophetic mission.

Second Part: The Danger of Living the Gospel

But what brought us together on this day? Why are we in Apopa under the sun? You all, brothers (and sisters), we are very comfortable here in the shade! What brought us together in Apopa, from all corners of the Vicariate and even other communities outside the borders of our Vicariate is the case of Father Mario. It is an ecclesiastical event. The Church cannot remain silent. She cannot stay out of this matter. We feel affected.

We hear it among the people: What are you going to do? All over the countryside, simple people, humble people, those who would listen to Father Mario on the air, were asking us—"What are you going to do?!" Well, here we are! At least to give a symbolic and official demonstration of protest from the Church, from our communities, from this part of the Church Archdiocese. He was a priest in the local Church of San Salvador and specifically here, he was the pastor of Apopa, thus having a mission on behalf of the Church in this community. Surprisingly he was expelled, after a chain of events that resulted in moral violence, with accusations that were never proven in trial, and with no opportunity to defend himself. Against all human rights of all the civilized nations of the world. I regret how his can happen in my country.

If Father Mario committed a crime, then try him in court and publicly tell us the verdict. Even Jesus of Nazareth was given a public, albeit rigged, trial, on the night between Holy Thursday and Good Friday. Not even this was granted to poor Father Mario.

They tell me that he was a foreigner! Father Mario, a foreigner?! Certainly, and from Latin America. I wonder how in Latin America, discovered by Columbus, where we are all kneaded together with coffee with milk as well as blood, we can be foreigners! Can we be foreigners anywhere? From Colombia… All that talking about being Hispanic on October 12, many children waving little flags and applauding with their teachers! The day of Hispanic heritage, the day of Latin America. What does that mean? He, a foreigner! But this is not the issue!

What is at stake is the fundamental question of being Christian today, of being a priest today in our country and on the continent that is suffering the hour of martyrdom. Whether or not to be faithful to the mission of Jesus under the real circumstances that we have to face in this country. This is a country where a poor priest or a poor catechist in our community can be falsely accused, threatened, taken away secretly in the middle of the night, possibly even attacked with a bomb. It happened. And if he is a foreigner, he will be kicked out. Many foreigners have been kicked out. But the fundamental question remains.

It is dangerous to be Christian in our midst! It is dangerous to be truly Catholic! It is practically illegal to be an authentic Christian here, in our country. Because out of necessity the world around us is rooted on an established disorder, in front of which the mere proclamation of the Gospel becomes subversive. That's the way it must be, it cannot be otherwise! We are chained by disorder, not order!

What happens is that the priest or the simple Christian who practices his faith according to the basic and simple guidelines of Jesus' message, must live faithfully between two demanding pillars: the revealed Word of God and the People. The same people, the great majority, the marginalized, the sick who cry out, those who are enslaved, those on the margins of culture—sixty percent illiterate—those who are alienated in a thousand ways, those who have been living in a feudal system for centuries. In some places in our country they do not own their land nor their lives. They must climb on the *conacaste* trees – not even those belong to them, not even the *conacaste* trees! The *chiltota* birds can fly up the trees and build their nests high in the branches. The poor Salvadoran is a slave to this land, which belongs to the Lord, according to the Bible.

This man is indeed poor! The statistics for our little country are dreadful. We already said that in the country, in this country, there exists a fake democracy, in name only. A lot is said, mouths are filled with "democracy". The power of the people is the power of a minority, not of the people! Let's not fool ourselves! The statistics for our country are dreadful in terms of public health, culture, crime rate, subsistence of the majority of the population, and possession of the land. We cover it all up with false hypocrisy, with magnificent deeds.

Woe to you, hypocrites, who pay lip service and call yourselves catholic, inside, you are nothing but evil filth! You are Cains and you crucify the Lord when he goes by the name of Manuel, the name of Luis, the name of Chabela, the name of the humble field worker!

"Our people are hungry for the real God and are hungry for bread" was correctly said during our Archdiocesan Pastoral Week. No privileged minority in our country has reason to exist in a Christian way by itself, but rather to serve the large majorities who form the Salvadorian people. We have no reason to exist as religious minorities, as an elite aware of our Christianity, including our lay leaders and established ministers, or as minorities that hold political, economic or social power. They have no reason to exist, but to serve the people!

Third Part. Fr. Mario Persecuted, like Jesus of Nazareth.

Going back to the case of Father Mario, those of us who met him, here in Apopa and other places, can say that he was a good and simple man. We would listen to him during our meetings of the priests in the Vicariate. His message was clean and clear like that of Jesus. He perfectly fulfilled his ministry within the limits that the priesthood is given by the Church. He did not go beyond these functions. He did not join a guerrilla group, he did not lead any organized political group. What he did was to speak the Word of the Lord, clearly and plainly, with his usual warmth. With no arrogance. And, in his parish, he tried to galvanize the different groups with the values of the Gospel.

He wanted the people in his parish to stop being simple followers of dead traditions, merely burying wood carved images year after year, but rather be the true worshippers of the living God, the followers of the Lord who is present in each one of the brothers who walks down the street in Apopa, in the market place, the workplace, the bus, the factory, the countryside.

He refused in the middle of the patron saint festivities—as a prophet, but both gently and firmly—he refused—I am saying—in this parish temple, in the middle of the patron saint festivities, to be surrounded by the selling stands of the poor women, who were tied with rope and brought there, like slaves, and surrounded him. He said: Saint Catalina de Apopa cannot be honored in such a hypocritical and stupid way. Brothers, if Jesus of Nazareth saw this he would say: "this is what I did." Father Mario also has done it.

I greatly fear, my dear brothers and friends, that very soon the Bible and the Gospel will not be able to enter through our borders. We will only get the book covers, because all the pages are too subversive. Subversive against sin, of course! In this context, it is interesting to see the avalanche of imported sects and of the slogans proclaiming freedom of religion, that are spreading around. Freedom of religion, freedom of religion! Freedom of religion so that they can bring us a false god. Freedom of religion so that they can bring us a god who is up in the clouds, sitting on a hammock. Freedom of religion so that they can introduce us to a Christ who is not the true Christ. It is false and it is serious!

I greatly fear, brothers that if Jesus of Nazareth returned, like that time, down from Galilee to Judea, that is, from Chalatenango to San Salvador, I dare say that this time he would not get as far as Apopa with his sermons and actions. I believe that they would arrest him sooner, by Guazapa. There they would take him prisoner and put him in jail… [the power is sabotaged and he is left without microphone.] Do not be upset… ! There is something else here to make my voice resound until the mountains! [Big applause as he continues with a megaphone.]

Therefore, dear brothers, I fear that if Jesus tried to cross the border, there by Chalatenango, they would not let him enter! They would arrest him by Apopa. Who knows if he even would make it as far as Apopa, right?! Or rather by Guazapa, tough on him! They would bring him in in front of many Supreme Courts for being unconstitutional and subversive. They would accuse the man-God, the prototype of man, of being an agitator, a foreign Jew, of stirring up exotic and strange ideas, contrary to "democracy," that is contrary to the minority. Ideas that are contrary to God, because they are; they are the clan of Cains.

Without a doubt, brothers, they would crucify him again. Perhaps, God forbid, I would also be among those who crucify him. Without a doubt, brothers, we will crucify him again, because we prefer a Christ of the mere gravediggers. Many prefer the Christ of the mere gravediggers. A mute Christ, without a mouth to be paraded on the streets. A muzzled Christ. A Christ made to our liking and according to our miserable interests. This is not the Christ of the Gospel! This is not the young Christ of thirty-three, who gave his life for humanity's noblest of causes!

My brothers, some people want a god up in the clouds. They do not want this Jesus of Nazareth, who is a stumbling block for the Jews and foolishness to the pagans. They want a god who does not question them, who lets them stay in their established order, and who does not utter these dreadful words: "Cain, what have you done with your brother Abel?" We must not take anybody's life. We must not hold our foot down on anybody's neck to dominate and humiliate him. As Christians we must be willing to give our lives for a just order, to save others, for the values of the Gospel.

Dear brothers: You probably read in the press that our humble Archbishop—who soon will no longer be Archbishop—our humble Archbishop, who, like our priests, has his own weaknesses and faults, just yesterday was harshly attacked by a group of Cains, who call themselves Catholics. He was publicly called a "communist" by an obstinate minority, because of his simple Pastoral Letters based on the Gospel.

Newspapers in our country, our own newspapers, have publicly attacked Church documents, such as Vatican II and, with incredible impudence, even [Pope] Paul VI, was attacked internationally in the high finance circles of the Empire: Wall Street. He was condemned saying that, in his famous encyclical On the Progression of Peoples, he supported a "reheated Marxism." It is the usual scandal, that occurs when the Gospel is announced and in a special way connected to its practice.

Mario Bernal, you are already far from us! We found out that they sent you back to Colombia via Guatemala, as the persecutors are linked together in every nation. Your strength, Father Mario, was the Gospel, and, at the same time, it was your weakness. In the same way, our strength is neither in the weapons, nor in the armies, nor in the G3, and not even the legions of angels, as Jesus told Pontius Pilate.

Mario, you triumphed in your weakness! And your enemies, who are also those of the Gospel, have been defeated. Because they are irrational, and with their irrationality they want to cover up the sun of truth, that cannot be covered with a finger or with brute strength. Your voice, Mario, will resonate through the valleys and the mountains of our countryside. Your exile joins the martyrdom of the Church in different nations of Latin America.

Last year a young priest, Colombian like you, Father Ivan, was brutally murdered with another North American priest and group of peasants, by a group of landowners in Olancho, Honduras. They were buried with a tractor, fifteen meters deep down a well. It was not many years ago, six maybe, that another Colombian, Father Héctor Gallego, was captured in the middle of the night in his small shack, in Santa Fe de Veraguas, Panama. That was the last that was heard about him. They threw him in the ocean, in the middle of the night.

He was helping the peasants working in a cooperative, in a network of cooperatives. In that way he was helping them put the Gospel into practice. That same type of people recently killed a Salesian priest and a Jesuit who had defended the indigenous people of Brazil. In Paraguay, an irrational dictator has exiled a number of priests. The list goes on. Here, among us, the list grows with those who are expelled from our country. A few days ago one of our brothers, Juan José Ramírez, was run over. They are not even expelling him, because they are treating his injuries! For defending the humble and the poor.

Dear Mario. When Pope Paul arrived to your land, Colombia, that is also our land, after he got off the plane, he knelt down and kissed the ground. It was the year 1968, and he talked from your land of Colombia to all the peasants of Latin America on the Day of Development, August 23, 1968. On the eve of that day, the bishops from the entire continent met and proclaimed "the freedom of God's children, in particular those oppressed on the continent."

These are the Pope's words, Mario, what if they were repeated around here…! You said the same words in different ways and they expelled you from the country. The Pope talks to the peasants in a special language:

> We love you with predilection, and together with us, always remember and hold present that the Holy Mother Catholic Church loves you, in spite of her sins and weaknesses. Because we know the conditions of your existence, conditions of misery for many, some below the basic necessities of human life. Now you are listening to us, in silence, beloved peasants, but we hear the shout that rises from your suffering and from the majority of humanity. We cannot ignore you. We want to support your cause, that is the cause of the humble, the simple people. We know that the economic and social development has been unequal in the great continent of Latin America, and while it favored those who promoted it at first, it has neglected the large native populations, almost always abandoned to live under ignoble conditions, often

harshly treated and exploited. We know that now, brothers and sisters, you realize that your social and cultural conditions are inferior and you are anxious to reach a better distribution of wealth and a better recognition of the importance that you deserve, given how many of you live in the continent, and of your rightful position in society. We believe that you know how the Catholic Church, in spite of her weaknesses, has defended your fate; the popes that came before us, have defended it with their social encyclicals; the Ecumenical Council, that includes three thousand bishops, has also defended it and we have sponsored your cause in the Encyclical on the Development of Peoples. But today, dear country people, the problem has become more serious because you are now aware of your needs and your suffering, and like many others in the world, you cannot endure and tolerate that these conditions last forever and no solution is found.

This is what the Pope says, Father Mario! This is what you said on the radio. This is what the Church documents say, and this is what the Salvadoran Church is saying. Unfortunately this is not allowed, this is not legal.

Padre Mario: These communities, those of Apopa and the surrounding Christian communities in the Vicariate, the brothers and sisters who have come, who have wanted to come from other parts of the country, of the local Church, we are all going to celebrate this Eucharist, that is the ideal that we support.

Long tablecloths and a communal table for everybody, a seat for everybody. And Christ in the middle! He, who did not take anybody's life, but rather offered his own to the noblest cause. This is what He said: Raise your cup and toast in your love for me! Recall my memory, commit to building the Kingdom, that is the fraternity of a communal table, the Eucharist.

Then hopefully we will say: "Agreed, Mario!" May this be the motto of this Eucharist, as you asked us on the radio when you were discussing the Gospel: Agreed? Agreed! Then, do *we* agree? [raising his hand over the New Testament, "Agreed!" everybody calls out together raising their hands.] Well, as we agree, let's say the Apostles Creed with our Church, which is agreeing with Father Mario, there in Bogotá, where they have thrown him. And let's enter the wave of the Holy Spirit celebrating this Eucharist. I believe in God, the Father...

ACKNOWLEDGEMENTS

Primary Translator: Irene Bubula-Phillips, Santa Clara University
Additional Translators: Olga Pavisich-Ryan, Carlos Duran S.J., Jake Schneider
Additional Contributor: Ana María Pineda, R.S.M.
Project Editor: Anthony Ferrari (Santa Clara University, class of 2015)
Published on Santa Clara University website, March 24, 2015.
https://www.scu.edu/ic/media--publications/articles/article-stories/a-life-of-faith-and-courage.html

BIBLIOGRAPHY

Arzobispo de Santiago, *Mons. Óscar Romero, Nadie Muere para Siempre*. Chile: Vicaria de la Solidaridad, 1980.

Brackley, D. "Crosses and Resurrections: Good News from Central America," *Thinking Faith*. February 18, 2009. http://www.thinkingfaith.org/articles/20090218_1.htm.

Brockman, James R., *Romero: A Life*. New York: Orbis Books, 1989.

— "The Spiritual Journey of Oscar Romero," *Spirituality Today*, Vol. 42 No. 4, Winter 1990, 303-322. http://www.spiritualitytoday.org/spir2day/904242brock.html.

— "Pastoral Teaching of Archbishop Oscar Romero," *Spirituality Today*, Vol. 40 No. 2, Summer 1988. http://www.spiritualitytoday.org/spir2day/884022brockman.html.

Campbell-Johnston, Michael, *The Jesuit Martyrs of El Salvador*, Barbados, 2009.

Cardenal, Rodolfo, *Historia de una Esperanza, Vida de Rutilio Grande*. El Salvador: UCA Editores, 2002.

Carranza, Salvador, *Una Luz Grande Nos Brilló*. El Salvador: Tallares Gráficos, UCA, 2007.

— *Romero-Rutilio Vidas Encontradas*. El Salvador: UCA Editores, 1992.

Carranza, Salvador and Miguel Cavada Diez and Jon Sobrino, *XXV Aniversario de Rutilio Grande, Sus Homilías*. El Salvador: Tallares Gráficos, UCA, 2008.

Cavada, Miguel, *El Corazón de Monseñor Romero*. El Salvador: Tallares Gráficos, UCA, 2010.

— "Rutilio Grande Visto por Óscar Romero" *Cartas a las Iglesias* Año XXII, Nº 491-492, February 1-28, 2002. http://www.uca.edu.sv/publica/cartas/ci491.html#Romero.

Delgado, Jesús, *Óscar A. Romero Biografía*. El Salvador: University of Central America Editors, 2005.

— *Monseñor Romero: Sus cartas personales, pensamientos y consejos.* El Salvador: Impreso en Talleres de Imprenta Criterio, 2004.

Dennis, Marie and Renny Golden and Scott Wright, *Oscar Romero, Reflections on His Life and Writings.* New York: Orbis Books, 2000.

Diez, Zacarías and Juan Macho, *En Santiago de María Me Tope Con La Miseria.* El Salvador, UCA, 1995.

Erdozain, Plácido, *Archbishop Romero: Martyr of Salvador.* New York: Orbis Books, 1981.

Filochowski, Julian, "*Archbishop Romero: Bishop, Martyr and Patron of Justice and Peace.*" Lecture given at Aylesford Priory in Kent, England, 2005.

Grande, Rutilio, "Sermon at Apopa" *Cartas a las Iglesias* digital, Año 17, nú. 371, (February 1-15, 1997). Accessed 2013. http://www.uca.edu.sv/publica/cartas/ci371.html.

Greenan, Thomas, "*Archbishop Romero Lecture.*" Lecture given in Edinburgh, Glasgow, Leeds, Liverpool, and London, 2010.

Hernández Pico, Juan, "*Romero and the Social Gospel: The Challenge for Us Today.*" Lecture given at the Lauriston Jesuit Centre at Edinburgh, 2011.

Hodgson, Irene B., *Through the Year With Oscar Romero: Daily Meditations.* Cincinnati: St. Anthony Messenger Press, 2005.

López Vigil, Maria, *Muerte y Vida en Morazán, Testimonio de un Sacerdote.* El Salvador: UCA Editores, 2007.

López Vigil, Maria, *Monseñor Romero: Memories in Mosaic.* New York: Orbis Books, 2013.

Maier, Martin, "*The Last Shall Be the First, Oscar Romero and the Joy of the Gospel.*" Independent Catholic News, 2014. http://www.indcatholicnews.com/news.php?viewStory=24413, accessed 2014.

— *Monseñor Romero: Maestro de Espiritualidad.* El Salvador: UCA Editores, 2005.

Radcliffe, Timothy, "*A Disturbing Truth: the Church, the poor, and Oscar Romero.*" The 2013 Romero Memorial Lecture at the Westminster Abbey Institute, Manchester and Edinburgh, October 2013.

Romero, Oscar, *Archbishop Oscar Romero, a Shepherd's Diary.* Cincinnati: St. Anthony Messenger Press, 1993.

— "*Dedicated Love, Homily for the Funeral Mass of Father Rutilio Grande.*" Archbishop Romero Trust, March 14 1977. http://www. romerotrust.org.uk/homilies-and-writings/homilies/dedicated-love

— *Monseñor Oscar A. Romero, Su Diario.* El Salvador: Impreso en Talleres de Imprenta Criterio, 2000.

— *The Violence of Love.* New York: Orbis Books, 1988.

— *Voice of the Voiceless, The Four Pastoral Letters and other Statements.* New York: Orbis Books, 2005.

Sánchez, Carlos Isidro, Jon Sobrino, and José Ricardo Urioste, *La Espiritualidad de Monseñor Romero: Servir Con La Iglesia.* El Salvador: Talleres de Imprenta Criterio, 2000.

Sobrino, Jon, *Monseñor Romero.* El Salvador: UCA Editores, 2004.

— *Spirituality of Liberation.* New York: Orbis Books, 1998.

— "Rutilio y Romero. Fuentes de Esperanza." *Carta a las Iglesias* Año XXII, N°491-492, February 1-28, 2002. http://www.uca.edu.sv/publica/cartas/ci491.html.

Urioste, Ricardo, "*Memories of Archbishop Oscar Romero.*" Lecture given in Lauriston Jesuit Centre, 2007.

Wright, Scott, *Oscar Romero and the Communion of the Saints: A Biography.* New York: Orbis Books, 2009.